MARY BERRY'S

RECIPES FROM HOME & ABROAD

BLACK CAT

Home economist
Rosemary Wadey
Stylist
Roisin Nield
Photographers
Martin Brigdale (England, France, Switzerland, Italy, America, India and Japan)
Peter Myers (China, Greece, Germany, Holland, Mexico)
Prelims
Paul Kemp
Line drawings
Sarah Gay-Wolfendale
Line illustrations
Anne Haweson

Our thanks to the following for the loan of props or food:
Dutch Dairy Bureau
Kiku Japanese Resaurant
Mitsukiku
Sharwoods and Co. Ltd.
Trend Interiors, Richmond
Youngs Seafoods Ltd.
Elizabeth David (Kitchenware)
Worlds End Tiles

First published in Great Britain as *Mary Berry's Recipes from Home and Abroad* 1981 by Macdonald & Co (Publishers) Ltd in association with Thames Television Limited
Reprinted 1989 by Macdonald & Co (Publishers) Ltd under the Black Cat imprint

Macdonald & Co (Publishers) Ltd,
66-73 Shoe Lane,
London EC4P 4AB

a member of Maxwell Pergamon Publishing Corporation plc

ISBN 0-7481-0210-8

Printed and bound by Novograph, Spain

CONTENTS

ENGLAND

HOLLAND

GERMANY

SWITZERLAND

FRANCE

Samuel
PALE
ALE

ENGLAND

Traditionally, the best of English cooking is plain and hearty and eaten at home. It is perhaps because eating out is not so much part of the English way of life as it is in, say, Italy and France, that until recently foreigners have thought of English food as stodgy and indigestible. Thankfully things are now changing and enterprising English restaurateurs are setting up all over the country to make good use of fresh local produce. Though traditional favourites such as fish and chips will never disappear from our menus, we are becoming more conscious of the need for a varied diet. Lastly, England is famous for cakes: in the North of England high tea is still a main meal, and this is perhaps why baking has retained its great popularity.

Old-Fashioned Lentil Soup

8 oz (225 g) lentils (orange or brown)
1 large onion
2 sticks celery
2 potatoes
1 oz (25 g) bacon fat
2 pints (1 l) chicken stock
Bacon or ham bone if available
About 1 teaspoon salt
Ground black pepper

Cook's Tip *A nutritious warming soup. It works well with split peas instead of lentils.*

Wash the lentils, put in a bowl and cover with cold water. Leave to soak overnight.

Drain the lentils and discard the water. Chop the onions, slice the celery and cube potatoes. Melt the fat in a large saucepan and add vegetables. Sauté gently for 10 minutes, without browning. Add lentils, stock, ham bone and seasoning, and bring to the boil. Cover the saucepan and simmer for one hour or until lentils are tender.

Raised Derby Pie, served with pickles

Lift out ham bone and puree the soup in a blender, taste and check seasoning. Rinse out the saucepan, return soup and reheat. Serve piping hot. Serves 6.

Salmon Mousse

1 rounded tablespoon gelatine
4 tablespoons cold water
10½ oz (298 g) condensed consommé soup
½ pint (300 ml) double cream, whisked until just thick
¾ pint (450 ml) good mayonnaise
Juice of 1 lemon
12 oz (350 g) cooked flaked salmon
Salt and black pepper
1 tablespoon chopped parsley

To cook the salmon, cover with water, add a slice of lemon, salt and pepper and bring to the boil slowly. Simmer for 4 minutes and then leave to cool in the water preferably overnight.

Put the gelatine in a small bowl or cup with the water and leave to soak for 5 minutes to form a sponge. Stand in a pan of simmering water and stir until dissolved and the gelatine is clear.

Put the undiluted consommé in a bowl and stir in the gelatine. Blend the cream, mayonnaise and lemon juice together in another bowl, then fold in the flaked salmon and three quarters of the consommé, taste and check seasoning.

Pour into a 2½-3 pint (1.4-1.7 l) dish and leave to set. Stir the parsley into the remaining consommé and carefully spoon over the mousse. It may be necessary to warm the consommé slightly if it has set.

Return to the refrigerator and chill until required. If frozen, thaw for six hours. Serves 10 as a first course.

Cook's Tip *This makes a little salmon go a long way. You could use pink trout instead.*

Hot Grapefruit

2 large grapefruit
4 tablespoons light soft brown sugar
½ level teaspoon ground ginger or cinnamon
Large knob of butter

Cut the grapefruit in half and cut around each half to loosen the flesh. Cut between the segments and remove pith and white skin.

Mix the sugar with the ginger or cinnamon and sprinkle over the grapefruit, then dot with butter.

Place under a moderate grill and grill lightly until the sugar has melted and the grapefruit are hot through. Serve at once.

Cook's Tip *This starter is quick to prepare and makes a useful standby if guests arrive unexpectedly.*

Raised Derby Pie

The pastry used in this pie is different from the usual shortcrust. However it is very easy to do and is wonderfully crisp.

Filling:
3½ lb (1.5 kg) chicken
8 oz (225 g) pork sausagemeat
8 oz (225 g) bacon pieces, finely minced or chopped
1 tablespoon chopped fresh mixed herbs
1 teaspoon ground mace
2 teaspoons salt, according to saltiness of the bacon
Ground black pepper
6 small hard-boiled eggs, shelled
Beaten egg and milk to glaze

Pastry:
12 oz (350 g) plain flour
1 teaspoon salt
5 oz (150 g) lard
¼ pint and 2 tablespoons water

Grease an 8 inch (20 cm) loose-bottomed cake tin.

First carve off the leg and thigh from the chicken, then remove the skin and bone. Take the meat off the rest of the bird, discard the skin and make stock from all the bones.

Cube all the chicken and put in a bowl with the bacon, herbs, sausagemeat and seasoning.

Now make the pastry: Put flour and salt in a bowl. Put lard and water into a pan and allow the lard to melt and the water to boil. Make a well in the centre of the flour and pour on all the liquid, mixing quickly with a wooden spoon or fork until it becomes a smooth dough.

When cool enough to handle take two thirds of the dough and roll into a circle 3 inches (7.5 cm) larger than the tin. Slip this into the tin and with the hands work it evenly up the sides until it stands about 3 inches (7.5 cm) from the base.

Put half the meat mixture in the tin, level and make six dents in the mixture and arrange the eggs in them. Cover with the remaining meat mixture and flatten.

Brush the inside of the pastry top with beaten egg and milk. Roll out the remaining pastry to a circle just over 8 inches (20 cm) for the lid and lift on top of the pie, press the edges firmly together and flute using the thumb and first finger of the right hand and the index finger of the left hand, or just press with the prongs of a fork. Make four holes in the top of the pie and decorate with pastry leaves if liked. Brush with beaten egg and bake in the oven at 425 deg.F, 220 deg.C, gas mark 7 for 45 minutes. Reduce the heat to 350 deg.F, 180 deg.C, gas mark 4 for a further 30 minutes. Remove from oven and leave to cool in the tin. Chill the pie overnight before turning out and serving sliced in wedges. Serves 8 to 10.

Salmon Mousse

Old English Rabbit Pie

2½ oz (62 g) butter
1 lb (450 g) diced boneless rabbit meat (or chicken)
8 oz (225 g) onions, chopped
12 oz (350 g) carrots, diced
2 oz (50 g) flour
1 pint (600 ml) milk
Salt and pepper

Suet crust:
6 oz (175 g) self-raising flour
3 oz (75 g) shredded suet
A little water to mix

Cook's Tip *Rabbit is readily available in freezer centres and at some butchers. However, chicken can be used as an alternative.*

Heat the oven to 350 deg.F, 180 deg.C, gas mark 4.

Melt the butter in a frying pan and fry the rabbit and onions for 3 to 4 minutes. Add the carrots and cook for a further minute. Stir in the flour and cook for a minute, then add the milk and bring to the boil, stirring until thickened. Season to taste and turn into 3½ pint (2 l) oven-proof casserole. Cover and cook in the centre of the oven for 45 minutes.

Place the flour and suet in a bowl with a little salt and mix to a soft, but not sticky dough with water. Roll out to about ½ inch (1.25 cm) thickness to cover the casserole.

Take the casserole from the oven and increase the heat to 400 deg.F, 200 deg.C, gas mark 6. Remove the lid from the casserole and place the suet crust on top of the rabbit. Return to the oven and bake for a further 30 minutes or until the top is crisp and golden brown. Serves 4.

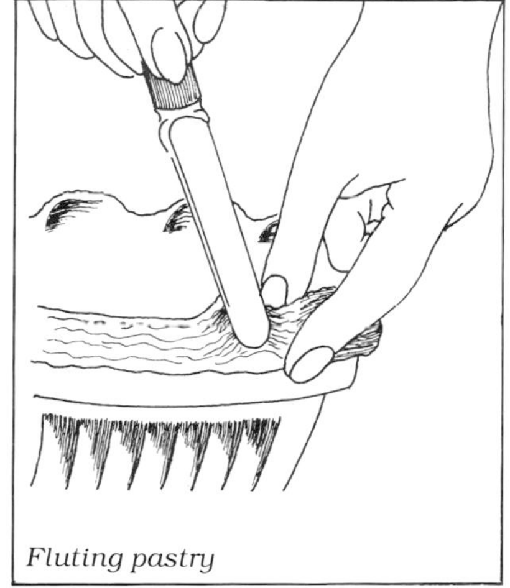

Fluting pastry

Wiltshire Bacon Bake

1 lb (450 g) potatoes
8 oz (225 g) cooked ham or bacon
6 oz (175 g) mushrooms
2 oz (50 g) butter
2 oz (50 g) flour
1 pint (600 ml) milk
1 chicken stock cube
3 hardboiled eggs, chopped
Salt and pepper
2 oz (50 g) full flavoured Cheddar cheese, grated
1 oz (25 g) Parmesan cheese, grated (optional)

Cook's Tip *The last pieces of a joint of ham or bacon are often sold off quite cheaply at delicatessen counters and are ideal for a dish like this. You can also use leftover cooked potatoes.*

Boil the potatoes in their skins until cooked, then drain, peel and slice. Cut the ham or bacon into neat cubes and dice the mushrooms.

Melt the butter in a large saucepan, stir in the flour and cook gently for two minutes. Add the milk and stock cube and bring to the boil, stirring until thickened and the stock cube has dissolved.

Add the potato, ham, mushrooms and eggs, mix well and season to taste. Turn into a 3 pint (1.7 l) ovenproof dish and sprinkle with cheese. Place under a moderate grill until golden brown and hot through.

If the pie has been made in advance put it in the oven at 375 deg.F, 190 deg.C, gas mark 5 for 25 to 30 minutes.

Serve hot with French bread and a green salad. Serves 4 to 6.

Norfolk Pork

6 lean pork chops
About 1 tablespoon seasoned flour
12 oz (350 g) onions, chopped
12 oz (350 g) Bramley apples, peeled, cored and cut in chunks
1 level teaspoon salt
Ground black pepper
½ pint (300 ml) cider

Remove the rind and excess fat from the pork chops and keep on one side.

Put the seasoned flour in a bag and drop each chop in one at a time to lightly coat the surface.

Put the pieces of fat in a large frying pan and heat gently until the base of the pan is lightly coated with the fat, then discard them. Add the chops to the pan and brown on both sides; lift out onto a plate.

Add the onion to the pan and fry gently in the remaining fat for five minutes, then add the apple and cook for a couple of minutes, stirring. Add salt and plenty of ground black pepper. Put half the apple and onion in a shallow 2 pint (a good litre) ovenproof dish, lay the chops on top, then cover with the rest of the onion mixture and pour over the cider.

Bake uncovered in the oven at 350 deg.F, 180 deg.C, gas mark 4 for about one hour.

If this dish has been prepared in advance and put in the refrigerator it will require about 1¼ hours in the oven. Serves 6.

Cook's Tip *This recipe is a good way of using up windfall apples.*

Beef Parcels

4 slices silverside

Stuffing:
1 oz (25 g) butter
2 oz (50 g) bacon, chopped
2 oz (50 g) mushrooms, chopped
2 oz (50 g) fresh white breadcrumbs
1 level tablespoon chopped parsley
Salt and ground black pepper

Sauce:
1 oz (25 g)) dripping
1 oz (25 g) flour
½ pint (300 ml) beef stock
2 tablespoons sherry
6 sticks celery, sliced

Trim the meat and then place each piece in turn between wetted greaseproof paper and beat flat with a rolling pin. The wet paper helps to stop the meat sticking to the rolling pin.

Prepare the stuffing: Melt the butter in a small pan and fry the bacon and mushrooms gently for 2 to 3 minutes. Stir in the rest of the ingredients and mix well. Divide the stuffing into four and place one portion on each slice of meat, roll up and tie with fine string or fix with wooden cocktail sticks.

Melt the dripping in a large saucepan and fry the beef to brown on all sides, lift out and place on one side. Stir the flour into the dripping remaining in the pan and cook for two minutes. Add stock and sherry and bring to the boil, stirring until thickened. Add the celery and plenty of salt and pepper.

Return the meat to the pan, cover with a tightly fitting lid and simmer gently for 1½ to 2 hours or until tender.

Taste and check seasoning, arrange the parcels on a warm dish and remove the string or cocktail sticks. Spoon over the sauce. Serves 4.

Cook's Tip *These parcels may also be cooked in a slow cooker, allowing about 30 minutes on high and then turning down to low for about 6 hours.*

Savoury Pancakes

Filling:
2 rashers streaky bacon, chopped
1 lb (450 g) minced beef
1 onion, chopped
1 stick celery, chopped
½ oz (12.5 g) flour
¼ pint (150 ml) beef stock
2 level tablespoons tomato puree
1 level teaspoon salt
Black pepper
A little thyme

Sauce:
1 oz (25 g) butter
1 oz (25 g) flour
½ pint (300 ml) milk
½ level teaspoon made English mustard
Salt and pepper
4 oz (100 g) grated Cheddar cheese

8 unsugared pancakes (see p.11)

For the filling: Put the bacon, beef, onion and celery in a pan and cook gently for 5 to 10 minutes to allow the fat to run out. Stir in the flour, then add the stock and bring to the boil, stirring. Add the remaining ingredients, cover and simmer for 30 to 40 minutes or until tender.

Spread the pancakes flat and divide the meat mixture between them. Roll up and lay in a single

Beef Parcels

layer in a shallow ovenproof dish and keep warm.

Make the sauce: Melt the butter in a small saucepan, stir in the flour and cook for a minute. Blend in the milk and bring to the boil, stirring until thickened, and simmer for 2 minutes. Add the mustard and seasoning and 3 oz (75 g) cheese. Stir until the cheese has melted.

Spoon over the pancakes and sprinkle with the remaining cheese. Place under a moderate grill until the top is golden brown and bubbling. Serve at once with a green salad and crispy French bread. Serves 4.

If you have made this dish earlier in the day, reheat it in the oven at 375 deg.F, 190 deg.C, gas mark 5 for 20 to 30 minutes.

Variation

If desired the pancakes may be stacked. Take a deep round ovenproof dish and put one pancake at the bottom. Cover with a thin layer of meat filling. Add another pancake on top and continue to sandwich the filling and pancakes together, finishing with a pancake. Pour over the cheese sauce, sprinkle with the remaining cheese and bake as above for 25 minutes or until hot through and golden brown and bubbling.

Fennel With Lemon Butter

Such a delicious vegetable. When raw it has a distinct aniseed flavour which is more subtle when cooked.

4 fennel heads
Salt and pepper
Butter
Juice of 1 lemon

Heat the oven to 350 deg.F, 180 deg.C, gas mark 4.

Cut each fennel into six wedges and arrange in an ovenproof serving dish seasoning well between layers. Dot with butter and pour over the lemon juice.

Cover with a lid or piece of foil and bake in the oven for about one hour or until the fennel is tender. Serves 6.

Cook's Tip *Always buy the whitest bulbs possible, as the green ones taste bitter.*

Classic Pancakes

Caster sugar
4 oz (100 g) plain flour
Good pinch salt
1 egg
½ pint (300 ml) milk and water mixed half and half
1 tablespoon vegetable or corn oil
Oil for frying
1 lemon

Sprinkle a little caster sugar onto a sheet of greaseproof paper and put on one side.

Measure the flour and salt into a mixing bowl and make a well in the centre. Add the egg and gradually stir in half the milk and water. Using a whisk, blend in the flour from the sides of the bowl. Beat well until smooth. Stir in the remaining liquid and the oil.

Heat an 8 inch (20 cm) frying pan and a little oil. When it is hot pour off any excess and spoon about two tablespoons of the batter into the pan. Tip and rotate the pan so that the batter spreads out evenly and thinly covers the base. Cook the pancakes for about one minute until pale brown underneath.

Turn over with a palette knife, or wooden spatula if using a non-stick pan, or toss, then cook for another minute until pale golden brown. Invert the pancake onto the sugared paper and roll up. Place on a hot serving dish and put this over a steaming pan to keep warm while you make the remaining pancakes.

Serve with lemon wedges. Makes 8 to 10 pancakes.

Cook's Tip *To freeze the pancakes leave them until cold. Freeze in stacks, wrapped in clear film, and keep for up to 3 months.*

Rich Fudge

A dark rich fudge, full of flavour.

8 oz (225 g) hard margarine
1 good tablespoon golden syrup
1 lb (450 g) granulated sugar
13½ oz (383 g) can condensed milk
1 teaspoon white distilled malt vinegar
1 teaspoon vanilla essence

Put the margarine and syrup in a saucepan and let the margarine melt. Add the sugar, stir well and bring to the boil slowly, stirring until the sugar has dissolved. Boil gently for 5 minutes.

Add the condensed milk, bring back to the boil and boil gently for 20 minutes, stirring continuously, otherwise the fudge will catch very easily.

Remove the pan from the heat,

add the vinegar and vanilla essence and beat well until the fudge starts to thicken. Turn into a greased 7 inch (17.5 cm) square tin and leave to set.

Cut into about 64 pieces and store in an airtight tin.

Victorian Christmas Cake

An easy but different and special cake. The dried fruit is soaked for 3 days in sherry which makes it very moist. This is not a really deep cake so don't expect it to rise to the top of the tin.

1 lb (450 g) mixed dried fruit including peel
4 oz (100 g) stoned raisins, chopped
4 oz (100 g) glacé cherries, quartered
¼ pint (150 ml) medium or sweet sherry
6 oz (175 g) soft margarine
6 oz (175 g) soft brown sugar, Muscovado or Barbados
Grated rind of 1 lemon
Grated rind of 1 orange
3 eggs
1 tablespoon black treacle
2 oz (50 g) blanched almonds, chopped
4 oz (100 g) plain flour
2 oz (50 g) self-raising flour
1 level teaspoon mixed spice

Put all the fruit in a bowl, pour over the sherry, cover and leave to soak for at least three days, stirring daily.

Put the margarine, sugar, lemon and orange rind, eggs, treacle and almonds in a bowl.

Sift together the flours and spice and add to the bowl, then mix until evenly blended. Stir in the soaked fruit and sherry.

Heat the oven to 300 deg.F, 150 deg.C, gas mark 2. Grease and line with greased greaseproof paper an 8 inch (20 cm) round cake tin and then put in the mixture and smooth the top flat.

Bake in the oven for two hours, then reduce the heat to 275 deg.F, 140 deg.C, gas mark 1 for a further 1¼ hours. Check the cake by piercing the centre with a warm skewer. If it comes out clean the cake is cooked. If not, cook for a further 15 minutes. If, during the cooking time, the cake seems to be getting too brown on top cover loosely with a sheet of foil.

Chocolate Cake, Lemon Butterfly Cakes and Brown Sugar Meringues

Coffee and Walnut Fudge Cakes

6 oz (175 g) soft margarine
6 oz (175 g) caster sugar
3 large eggs
2 oz (50 g) chopped walnuts
1 tablespoon coffee essence
6 oz (175 g) self-raising flour
1½ level teaspoons baking powder

Coffee fudge icing:
3 oz (75 g) soft margarine
8 oz (225 g) icing sugar, sieved
1 tablespoon milk
1 tablespoon coffee essence
2 oz (50 g) chopped walnuts

Heat the oven to 325 deg.F, 160 deg.C, gas mark 3 and grease and line with greased greaseproof a large tin 12 by 9 inches (30 by 22.5 cm).

Measure the margarine, sugar, eggs, walnuts and coffee essence into a large bowl and then sieve in the flour and baking powder. Beat well until smooth and blended.

Turn into the prepared tin, smooth the top and cook for 40 minutes or until well risen and shrinking away from the sides of the tin. The cake will spring back when pressed with the finger tips. Leave to cool in the tin.

For the icing: put the margarine, icing sugar, milk and coffee essence in a bowl and beat until smooth. Spread over the cake and sprinkle with walnuts. Leave to set. Cut into bars.

Lemon Butterfly Cakes

4 oz (100 g) soft margarine
4 oz (100 g) caster sugar
2 large eggs, beaten
Finely grated rind of 1 lemon
4 oz (100 g) self-raising flour
1 level teaspoon baking powder

Butter cream:
2 oz (50 g) soft margarine
4 oz (100 g) icing sugar
About 2 tablespoons lemon juice

thoroughly blended.

Turn into the tins and then bake in the oven for 25 to 30 minutes. When cooked the cake will spring back when lightly pressed with the finger.

Turn out, remove the paper and leave to cool on a wire rack. Sandwich the cakes together with cream.

For the icing: Melt the margarine in a small saucepan, stir in the cocoa and cook over a gentle heat for one minute. Remove from the heat and add the milk and icing sugar. Beat well to mix and then leave to cool, stirring occasionally, until the icing has thickened to a spreading consistency. Spread over the top of the cake and swirl attractively with a round bladed knife. Leave to set. Keep covered in the refrigerator.

Brown Sugar Meringues

Cook's Tip *Don't make the mistake of using all brown sugar as often the result will be rather sticky meringues.*

4 egg whites
4 oz (100 g) light soft brown sugar
4 oz (100 g) caster sugar
Whipping cream

Heat the oven to 200 deg.F, 100 deg.C, gas mark ¼ or Low. Line two baking sheets with silicone paper.

Place the egg whites in a large bowl and whisk on high speed with an electric or hand rotary whisk until they form soft peaks.

Sieve the two sugars together until evenly mixed. Add a teaspoonful at a time to the egg whites, whisking well after each addition until all the sugar has been added.

Using two dessertspoons, spoon the meringue out onto the baking sheets, putting ten meringues on each tray.

Bake in the oven for three to four hours until the meringues are firm and dry and will lift easily from the paper. They will be pale brown. Leave to cool.

Whisk the cream until thick and use to sandwich the meringue shells together. Makes 10 meringues.

Heat the oven to 400 deg.F, 200 deg.C, gas mark 6. Thoroughly grease 18 deep bun tins.

Place all the cake ingredients together in a bowl and beat well for two minutes until blended and smooth. Divide the mixture equally between the bun tins.

Bake in the oven for 15 to 20 minutes, until a pale golden brown. Turn out and leave to cool on a wire rack.

Now make the butter cream: Beat the margarine in a small bowl until soft and then add the icing sugar and lemon juice and continue to beat until the mixture is light and fluffy. Cut a slice from the top of each cake and cut in half; pipe or spoon a little of the butter cream into the centre of each cake. Arrange the cake wings in the centre of the butter cream and dust with a little extra icing sugar. Makes 18 butterfly cakes.

Good Basic Chocolate Cake

1 oz (25 g) cocoa
2 tablespoons hot water
4 oz (100 g) soft margarine
4 oz (100 g) caster sugar
2 large eggs
4 oz (100 g) self-raising flour
1 level teaspoon baking powder

Filling:
¼ pint (150 ml) whipping cream, whipped

Icing:
1½ oz (40 g) soft margarine
1 oz (25 g) cocoa, sieved
2 tablespoons milk
4 oz (100 g) icing sugar, sieved

Cook's Tip *Cocoa gives the strongest chocolate flavour and is less expensive than drinking chocolate or plain chocolate.*

Heat the oven to 350 deg.F, 180 deg.C, gas mark 4. Grease and line with greased greaseproof paper two 7 inch (17.5 cm) round sandwich tins.

Blend the cocoa with the hot water in a large bowl and leave to cool. Add the remaining cake ingredients to the bowl and beat with a wooden spoon for 2 to 3 minutes until the mixture is

HOLLAND

Dutch food is simple and satisfying and has been greatly enriched by the introduction of exotic spicy dishes from the Colonies. Dutch produce is renowned the world over. The Dutch cultivate their early vegetables as tenderly as their tulips and dress them with butter or butter-based sauces, sometimes spiced with nutmeg. Their cheese is known for its smooth delicate flavour. Edam is a favourite amongst slimmers for its low calorie count. Dutch bacon is another product that is exported to many countries – salting and smoking have been developed to a fine art. The Dutch serve a light meal of open sandwiches with cakes or biscuits and chocolate or coffee at midday and enjoy their main meal in the evening. Holland is famous for its lager, for Dutch gin and advocaat.

Uitsmijter

These are open sandwiches but the literal translation means 'bouncer'! Serve them for lunch.

A little butter
1 slice bread
1 slice cooked ham
2 eggs
1 tomato, sliced
A few lettuce leaves
A gherkin

Butter the slice of bread and lay the ham on top. Fry the eggs in butter and put on top of the ham. Garnish with tomato, lettuce and a gherkin. Serves 1.

Dutch Pea Soup

A thick, tasty warming soup that makes a nice light lunch in winter served with crispy bread and followed by Dutch cheese.

1 lb (450 g) green split peas
1 lb (450 g) gammon knuckle or 2 pigs' trotters
4 pints (2.3 l) water
8 oz (225 g) onions, chopped
4 sticks celery, chopped
4 potatoes, diced
2 leeks, sliced
1 tablespoon chopped parsley
Salt and pepper
1 oz (25 g) unsalted butter

Soak the peas and knuckle or trotters overnight in enough cold water to cover.

Drain in a colander and place peas and knuckle or trotters in a pan with water. Simmer uncovered for an hour. Add the vegetables, except the leeks, cover and simmer for 2½ hours.

Take the knuckle or trotters from the pan, remove the meat from the bones and return to the pan. Add leek, parsley and seasoning with the butter, bring back to the boil before serving. Serves 6 to 8.

Bitterballen

Delicious served hot with a mild mustard. Eat with drinks.

2 level teaspoons powdered gelatine
½ pint (300 ml) chicken stock
1 oz (25 g) butter
1 oz (25 g) flour
6 oz (175 g) cooked ham and veal, coarsely chopped
1 teaspoon chopped parsley
Salt and pepper
2 oz (50 g) flour for coating
3 oz (75 g) browned breadcrumbs
Deep fat or oil for frying

Put the gelatine with the chicken stock in a small saucepan and leave to soak for 2 minutes, then put over a gentle heat until the gelatine dissolves.

Melt the butter and stir in the flour and cook for a minute. Stir in the stock, bring to the boil, stirring, then simmer for 2 minutes. Stir in the meat and parsley and taste and check seasoning.

Wrap the mixture in a piece of foil and chill until firm.

Roll into small balls, dip in flour, then into the beaten egg and breadcrumbs. Fry in hot deep fat or oil until golden brown. Drain on kitchen paper. Makes about 30.

Dutch Croquettes

A tasty supper dish served with a crisp green salad.

2 rashers streaky bacon, chopped

Dutch Pea Soup with Gouda and Edam Cheeses

HOLLAND
GOUDA

4 oz (100 g) butter
4 oz (100 g) flour
½ pint (300 ml) milk
2 eggs, separated
8 oz (225 g) cooked chicken, finely chopped
1 rounded tablespoon chopped chives
Salt and pepper
¼ teaspoon nutmeg
2 teaspoons Worcestershire sauce
Browned breadcrumbs
Deep fat or oil for frying

Fry the bacon until crisp, lift out with a slotted spoon and drain on kitchen paper.

Melt the butter in a saucepan, add the flour and cook for a minute. Add the milk and bring to the boil, stirring to make a very thick sauce. Add the egg yolks, chicken, bacon, chives, seasoning, spice and Worcestershire sauce. Mix well, wrap in foil and chill overnight.

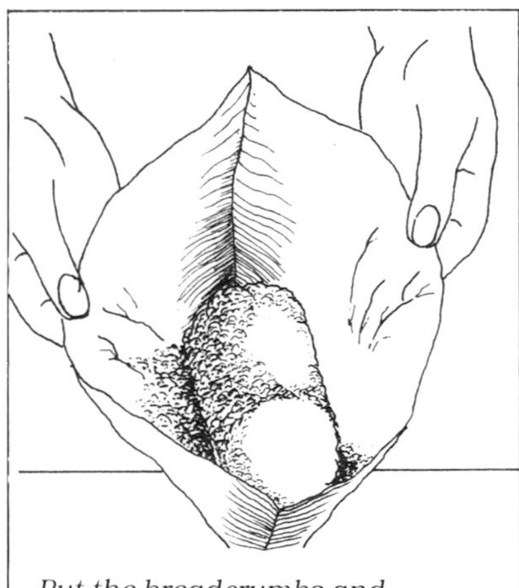

Put the breadcrumbs and croquettes in a bag and shake gently.

Shape into 12 croquettes, then coat in lightly whisked egg white and browned breadcrumbs. Fry in hot deep fat or oil until golden brown, drain on kitchen paper. Serve hot. Serves 4.

Nasi Goreng

This dish was brought to Holland from Indonesia when the Dutch ruled there. It is still very popular today.

1 lb (450 g) boned shoulder of pork
2 oz (50 g) pork dripping
8 oz (225 g) onions, sliced
8 oz (225 g) long-grain rice
8 oz (227 g) packet frozen mixed vegetables
4 tablespoons soy sauce
1 level teaspoon curry powder
Salt and pepper

Omelette:
1 egg
1 teaspoon cold water
Seasoning
Knob of butter
4 tomatoes

Cut the pork into ½ inch (1.25 cm) cubes. Heat the dripping in a large pan, add the pork and onions and fry quickly for 5 minutes. Reduce the heat, cover the pan and cook gently for 30 minutes, stirring occasionally.

Meanwhile cook the rice in fast-boiling salted water for about 12 minutes or as directed on the packet, drain well and rinse in warm water.

Cook the vegetables as directed on the packet and drain.

Stir the soy sauce, curry powder and seasoning into the pork with the rice and vegetables and mix thoroughly. Check seasoning and heat gently.

Using the omelette mixture make a flat pancake. Mix the egg and water together with seasoning to taste. Melt the butter in a small omelette pan and pour in the egg mixture. Cook gently undisturbed until the underside is golden brown, turn over and lightly brown second side. Slip out onto a plate and cut into strips. Pile the rice on a serving dish and arrange the omelette strips on top in a lattice, garnishing the dish with tomato wedges. Serves 4 to 6.

Botermoppen

6 oz (175 g) unsalted butter
Finely grated rind of ½ lemon
4 oz (100 g) caster sugar
8 oz (225 g) plain flour
1 oz (25 g) granulated sugar

Cook's Tip *No biscuit cutters are needed for this recipe. Make the shortbread into a long sausage shape. Chill, then cut off round slices and bake.*

Heat the oven to 325 deg.F, 160 deg.C, gas mark 3, and grease two or three large baking trays.

Cream the butter and lemon

Bitterballen

rind in a large bowl until soft. Beat in the sugar until light. Blend in the flour and mix until smooth. Using your hands, work the mixture together and divide into two equal portions. Roll both out to form two 6 inch (15 cm) sausages and roll them in the granulated sugar. Wrap in foil and chill in the refrigerator until firm.

Cut each sausage into about 16 slices and place on the baking trays allowing room for the biscuits to spread slightly. Bake in the oven for about 25 minutes or until pale golden brown at the edges. Lift off and leave to cool on a wire rack. Makes 32 biscuits.

Janhagel

Using the same basic Botermoppen mixture (see above) omit the lemon rind and instead add one level teaspoon of ground cinnamon. Press the mixture into a shallow 7 by 11 inch (17.5 by 27.5 cm) tin. Flatten with a knife, prick with a fork and then brush with a little beaten egg. Sprinkle the granulated sugar on top and then add approximately 1 oz (25 g) of flaked almonds.

Bake in the oven for about 40 minutes at 325 deg.F, 160 deg.C, gas mark 3.

Leave to cool in the tin for about 15 minutes and then cut into 16 fingers, lift out and finish cooling on a wire rack.

Orange Yoghurt Pudding

A light sweet pudding that's refreshing after a heavy meal. Children love it.

11 oz (300 g) can mandarin oranges
½ oz (12.5 g) powdered gelatine
2½ oz (62 g) caster sugar
1 lb (450 g) carton natural yoghurt
Finely grated rind and juice of a lemon
¼ pint (150 ml) double cream

Drain the juice from the mandarins, place in a small bowl with the gelatine and leave to soak for 3 minutes.

Place the bowl over a pan of hot water and leave until the gelatine dissolves, then stir in the sugar and leave to cool.

Put the yoghurt, lemon rind and juice in a large bowl and stir in the gelatine mixture. Leave until starting to set.

Lightly whip the cream and fold into the mixture with most of the mandarins. Pour into a serving dish and leave to set. Decorate with the remaining mandarin orange segments. Serves 6.

Nasi Goreng

Boterletter

Pastry:
6 oz (175 g) plain flour
2 oz (50 g) hard margarine, chilled
2 oz (50 g) butter, chilled
About 7 tablespoons cold water

Filling:
6 oz (175 g) ground almonds
6 oz (175 g) caster sugar
1 egg
Juice of ½ lemon
Almond essence

Cook's Tip *These ingredients can be bought ready-made, i.e. a large packet of puff pastry and 12 oz (350 g) almond paste.*

Put the flour into a mixing bowl and grate in the fats. Add just enough cold water to mix to a firm dough, using a sharp knife. On a lightly floured surface roll out the pastry to a strip ½ inch (1.25 cm) thick and 6 inches (15 cm) wide. Fold the pastry in three and give it a quarter turn to the left. Roll out again into a strip and fold in three. Wrap the pastry in greaseproof paper and chill in the refrigerator for 30 minutes.

Heat the oven to 425 deg.F, 220 deg.C, gas mark 7.

Roll out the pastry to a strip 6 by 30 inches (15 by 75 cm). Mix all the filling ingredients together to form a paste, roll into a sausage a little shorter than the pastry and place in the centre. Wrap the pastry around the almond paste, sealing the edges and ends with beaten egg. Form into the shape of a letter of the alphabet.

Glaze with a little beaten egg and bake in the oven for about 30 minutes or until golden brown on top.

Remove from the oven and leave to cool. Serve sliced with coffee.

GERMANY

The history of German cooking falls into two distinct phases. Before Napoleon, people had to rely on their ingenuity to make the best of what local produce was in season. Napoleon's armies brought with them the cuisine of France – local cooking adopted its methods and as transport improved, new ingredients were assimilated from abroad. Today Germany is still a country of hearty eating and strongly regional cooking. It is famous for its white wine, light beer, black bread, smoked hams and cheeses and piquant sausage, sauerkraut, thick soups and dumplings. These substantial foods often take the place of meat, which is not served every day because it is so expensive.
The Germans are not known for their puddings, but they make superb cakes and tarts which are decorated with thick cream.

Curried Apple Soup

A really unusual soup that also tastes delicious served chilled.

1 oz (25 g) butter
1 onion, finely chopped
1½ oz (40 g) flour
1 level tablespoon curry powder
1½ pints (900 ml) water
2 chicken stock cubes
1½ lb (675 g) cooking apples, peeled and roughly chopped
2 tablespoons redcurrant jelly
Juice of ½ lemon
Salt and pepper
¼ pint (150 ml) single cream

Melt the butter in a large saucepan, add the onion and fry slowly with the lid on for 10 minutes or until soft. Stir in the flour and curry powder and cook for a minute. Add water, stock cubes, apples, redcurrant jelly and lemon juice and bring to the boil, stirring. Simmer for 15 minutes. Leave the soup to cool slightly and then sieve or puree in a blender.

Rinse out the saucepan, return the soup to it and bring to the boil. Taste and check seasoning. If necessary, add a little extra stock to thin down the soup. Pour a little cream on top of each bowl of soup as it is served. Serves 6.

German Onion Tart, Sausages and Cheeses

Gulasch Soup

A filling soup that is full of meat and vegetables, best eaten in a bowl or dish.

1 lb (450 g) stewing steak
2 oz (50 g) dripping
1 lb (450 g) onions
1 level tablespoon paprika pepper
14 oz (397 g) can peeled tomatoes
2 beef stock cubes
1½ pints (900 ml) water
1 lb (450 g) potatoes, diced
2 green peppers, chopped
1-2 teaspoons salt
Pepper

Cut the meat into very small cubes. Melt the dripping in a large saucepan and fry the beef and onions for 10 minutes to lightly brown. Stir in the paprika pepper, tomatoes, stock cubes and water and bring to the boil, stirring.

Cover the pan and simmer for an hour, then add the potatoes and green pepper and continue cooking for a further 30 minutes or until the meat and vegetables are tender. Taste and check seasoning.

Serve very hot. Serves 6.

German Onion Tart

Onion tart may sound dull, but you will see from the photograph that it's anything but. Serve as a starter, or as a main course with salad.

For the dough:
6 tablespoons lukewarm water
Good pinch sugar
½ oz (12.5 g) dried yeast
8 oz (225 g) strong plain flour
2 oz (50 g) butter, melted
1 egg yolk
½ level teaspoon salt

For the filling:
1½ lb (675 g) onions, sliced
1½ oz (40 g) butter
3 eggs
¼ pint (150 ml) soured cream
1½ oz (40 g) plain flour
½ level teaspoon salt
Freshly ground black pepper
1 teaspoon caraway seeds (optional)
4 oz (100 g) streaky bacon

Curried Apple Soup

To make the dough: Put the lukewarm water in a bowl, stir in the sugar, then sprinkle on the yeast and leave to stand for 10 minutes or until it is frothy. Stir 4 tablespoons of the flour into the yeast mixture, cover and set aside in a warm place for 15 minutes.

Sift the remaining flour into a bowl, make a well in the centre and stir in the yeast mixture, cooled melted butter, egg yolk and salt. Beat well with a wooden spoon until the dough is well mixed. Add a little more milk if the dough looks very dry. Knead well with floured hands until the dough leaves the sides of the bowl clean. Cover the bowl with a cloth and put in warm place until dough has doubled in bulk.

Meanwhile make the filling: Put the onions and butter in a large frying pan and sauté gently for about 20 to 25 minutes until soft but not brown. Remove the pan from the heat. Blend the eggs, soured cream and flour together, add the salt and plenty of freshly ground black pepper and caraway seeds if used.

Roll out the yeast dough and line a 9 inch (22.5 cm), quite deep flan tin. Pour in the filling and smooth the top flat. Cut the bacon into small pieces and sprinkle over the top.

Bake in the oven at 400 deg.F, 200 deg.C, gas mark 6 for about 35 minutes when the top will be golden brown and set and the bread crust crisp. Serve warm. Serves 6 to 8.

Sweet and Sour Braised Steak

A hearty main meal, very nourishing on a cold winter's day.

3 lb (1.3 kg) piece of chuck steak
½ pint (300 ml) red wine
4 tablespoons malt vinegar
2 bayleaves
3 cloves
6 black peppercorns
2 carrots, sliced
1 onion, sliced
2 sticks celery, sliced
2 tablespoons oil
1 oz (25 g) flour
2 tablespoons tomato puree
2 tablespoons thin honey
2 oz (50 g) raisins
Salt and pepper

Place the piece of chuck steak in a china or glass bowl and add the wine, vinegar, herbs and vegetables. Cover and leave in the refrigerator for at least 24 hours, preferably 48.

Heat the oven to 325 deg.F, 160 deg.C, gas mark 3.

Put the oil in a frying pan and heat through, then add the meat and quickly brown on both sides. Lift out and place in a large casserole. Stir the flour into the fat remaining in the pan and cook for a minute. Add all the ingredients in the marinade and bring to the boil, stirring. Pour over the meat, cover the casserole with a tight-fitting lid and cook in the oven for 2 to 3 hours, the time will vary with the thickness of the meat. Lift the meat out onto a board, carve in slices and arrange on a serving dish.

Strain the marinade into a small saucepan, add the tomato puree, honey, raisins, salt and pepper and bring to the boil, stirring. Simmer for 2 minutes, taste and check seasoning and then strain over the meat. Serves 8.

Oxtail in Beer

2 oxtails
3 tablespoons dripping
2 oz (50 g) flour
1 pint (600 ml) beer
½ pint (300 ml) beef stock
Bouquet garni
Peeled rind of 1 lemon in a spiral
Juice of 1 lemon
2 tablespoons redcurrant jelly
2 tablespoons tomato puree
½ teaspoon gravy browning
1 teaspoon salt
Freshly ground pepper
8 oz (225 g) pickling onions, peeled and left whole

Cook's Tip *Cook this the day before it is needed, skim off surplus fat and reheat on the day.*

Cut the oxtail into 2 inch (5 cm)

lengths through the vertebrae. Remove the surplus fat and fry gently in an ovenproof dish in the melted dripping for about 30 minutes, or until brown all over.

Heat the oven to 300 deg.F, 150 deg.C, gas mark 2.

Remove the oxtail from the pan and if necessary add more dripping. Stir in the flour and cook for a few minutes. Add the beer and stock and bring to the boil stirring all the time until thick.

Add the remaining ingredients except the onions. Cover with a lid and cook in the oven for 5 hours, adding the onions during the last hour of the cooking time.

Taste and check seasoning and remove the bouquet garni and piece of lemon peel. Serves 6.

Bismark Herrings

A useful dish for entertaining because it is prepared in advance. Leaves you more time to enjoy your guests!

6 small herrings
About 1 pint (600 ml) vinegar
Salt
Cayenne pepper
2 onions, very finely sliced

Scale and clean the herrings and wash under plenty of cold running water. Lay them in a dish and pour over the vinegar, adding a little extra vinegar if necessary to cover the fish. Cover and leave in a cool place for 24 hours.

Lift the herrings from the vinegar and remove the heads and backbone. Cut each herring into two fillets and arrange in a serving dish, sprinkle with salt and cayenne pepper and thinly sliced onions. Cover and leave again for another 24 hours in a cool place before serving. Serves 6.

Apple Strudel

Apple Strudel

2 pieces strudel pastry, each
16 inches (40 cm) square
1½ oz (40 g) butter, melted
2 oz (50 g) white breadcrumbs

Filling:
1½ lb (675 g) cooking apples, peeled, cored and finely diced
3 oz (75 g) caster sugar
1 level teaspoon cinnamon
2 oz (50 g) sultanas
Grated rind of 1 lemon
2 oz (50 g) ground almonds

Cook's Tip *Most good delicatessen shops sell strudel pastry, which makes this dish so simple to make.*

Heat the oven to 400 deg.F, 200 deg.C, gas mark 6.

Lay the two pieces of strudel pastry flat on the table, brush with melted butter and sprinkle with most of the breadcrumbs.

Mix all the filling ingredients together and divide between the two pieces of strudel pastry leaving a ½ inch (1.25 cm) border.

Fold in these borders and then carefully roll up like a Swiss roll.

Place on a baking sheet, brush each with more melted butter and sprinkle with the rest of the breadcrumbs. Bake in the oven for 30 minutes brushing once or twice with more melted butter, until golden brown.

Leave to cool on the baking tray, then cut into slices, and lift onto a serving dish. If liked sprinkle with sieved icing sugar. This makes 2 small strudels and serves 6.

SWITZERLAND

The Swiss people fall into three groups because of the languages they speak: Italian, French and German. It is not surprising that their cooking often reflects these divisions. Switzerland is a land of dairy farming, producing rich alpine cream and a variety of hard cheeses. Emmenthal and Gruyère being the best known. These two go with the local wine to make Switzerland's most fabled dish: cheese fondue. Each region boasts the 'original' recipe, but whatever the variation, eating fondue is a delightful social occasion.

Other traditional meals are based on fresh, salt and smoked meats or freshwater fish. Zürich is especially famous for its creamed veal. The main course is often followed by the most lavish of fruit gâteaux, decorated with cream and chocolate.

Cream of Spinach Soup

2 oz (50 g) butter
1 medium onion, chopped
1 large clove garlic, crushed
1 lb (450 g) fresh spinach
2 chicken stock cubes
1½ pints (900 ml) hot water
1 level teaspoon salt
Freshly ground black pepper
Juice of ½ a lemon
A little ground nutmeg
¼ pint (150 ml) single cream

Cook's Tip *Tastes best with fresh spinach but if none is available substitute an 8 oz (225 g) pack of frozen leaf spinach.*

Melt the butter in a saucepan, add the onion and garlic and fry for 5 minutes until soft. Wash the spinach very well in several lots of fresh water and remove all the stalks.

Dissolve the stock cubes in the hot water and add to the saucepan with the spinach, seasoning, lemon juice and nutmeg and bring to the boil, stirring. Cover the pan and simmer for 15 to 20 minutes.

Puree the spinach in an electric blender or sieve and pour into a clean bowl.

Rinse out the saucepan and return the soup to it. Bring back to the boil. Taste and check seasoning and just before serving, stir in the cream but do not allow to boil. Serves 6.

Cheese Fondue, made with Emmenthal and Gruyère

Cheese Fondue

1 clove garlic
Scant ¾ pint (450 ml) dry white wine or cider
8 oz (225 g) Swiss Emmenthal cheese, grated
8 oz (225 g) Gruyère cheese, grated
1 oz (25 g) cornflour
Salt and ground black pepper
1 tablespoon kirsch

Peel and crush the garlic very finely. Pour all but about 4 tablespoons of the wine into a thick enamel or earthenware pan. Add the garlic and grated cheese and heat the mixture very slowly until all the cheese has dissolved. Do not allow to boil.

Blend the cornflour with the remainder of the wine to make a smooth paste. Add a little of the hot cheese mixture to the cornflour then add this to the pan. Carefully bring the fondue to the boil, stirring all the time until the mixture has thickened. Add salt and pepper to taste and stir in the kirsch. Serves 4.

Cook's Tip *Serve as soon as it is made with plenty of French bread cut into small pieces to dip in the hot fondue.*

Fondue Bourguignonne

Inviting friends for a fondue party is a fun idea; not only does it make sure that you enjoy yourself, but it keeps your friends busy cooking their own supper!

For each person you will need:
6-8 oz (175-225 g) rump steak *or*
6-8 oz (175-225 g) leg fillet of lamb
Sufficient vegetable oil for frying (enough to fill the fondue pot ⅓ full)

Cut the meat into cubes ready to fry in the oil on skewers.

Heat the oil on the hob of the cooker in the kitchen until a faint haze is rising, then transfer it to the fondue stove. Remember that the oil will heat up more quickly with a lid on the pan, but keep an eye on it because it should not become too hot. On no account leave it unattended. Mark the skewers with coloured tape or wool so that each guest will know which is his. Take the meat off the skewers or forks, then spear with a dinner fork. This avoids the chance of burning your lips.

Keep the oil hot by returning it to the cooker at intervals and not cooking more than six portions of meat at a time. Guests can time their own steak cubes as some will like their meat rare.

There is no need for potatoes, just serve crisp French bread with plenty of butter and a green salad. Serve a selection of sauces, that may be made in advance.

Veal Zurich, Rösti and Swiss Salad

Curried mayonnaise:
Blend 4 tablespoons mayonnaise with a little lemon juice, one teaspoon curry powder and one tablespoon very finely chopped mango chutney.

Mustard and dill:
Blend 4 tablespoons mayonnaise with one tablespoon Dijon mustard and a little chopped dill.

Egg and parsley:
Blend 4 tablespoons mayonnaise with one finely chopped, hard-boiled egg and one tablespoon chopped fresh parsley. Add a little curry powder if liked.

Chutney:
Blend 4 tablespoons mayonnaise with chopped chunky tomato chutney or just serve tomato chutney on its own.

Veal Zurich

A very traditional Swiss dish that I often make when entertaining. The sauce is really heavenly.

12 oz-1 lb (350-450 g) thinly sliced escalope of veal
1½ oz (40 g) butter
About 1 tablespoon oil
6 oz (175 g) white button mushrooms, sliced
1 medium onion, finely chopped
¼ pint (150 ml) dry white wine
½ pint (300 ml) double cream
Salt and pepper
Chopped parsley

Take each slice of veal and cut into pencil-thin strips.

Melt half the butter in a large shallow pan, add the oil and fry the meat for 2 to 3 minutes over a brisk heat. Lift out with a slotted spoon onto a plate. Add the mushrooms to the pan and toss in the remaining fat for a minute, lift out and add to the meat. Add the remaining butter to the pan with the onions and cook gently until golden brown.

Pour the wine into the pan, scrape off any sediment with a wooden spatula and mix well. Cook quickly until the wine has reduced to about 4 tablespoons.

Stir in the cream with the seasonings, veal and mushrooms and simmer for a minute. Taste and check seasoning.

Serve with Rösti scattered with parsley. Serves 4.

Swiss Steak

A great standby of mine and a really good family dish that looks after itself during cooking.

4 slices topside of beef, each weighing about 6 oz (175 g)
1½ oz (40 g) flour
1 level teaspoon salt
¼ level teaspoon pepper
1½ oz (40 g) dripping
2 large onions, finely sliced
2 sticks celery, sliced
8 oz (227 g) can tomatoes
2 level teaspoons tomato puree
1 teaspoon Worcestershire sauce
¼ pint (150 ml) beef stock

Heat the oven to 300 deg.F, 150 deg.C, gas mark 2. Cut each slice of beef in half.

Mix together the flour, salt and pepper. Toss the meat in the seasoned flour, pressing it gently so that most of the flour is used.

Melt the dripping in a pan and fry the meat quickly on all sides until it is browned. Lift out and put in an ovenproof casserole. Add the onion and celery to the dripping remaining in the pan and fry until golden brown. If there should be any seasoned flour left over, stir it into the vegetables and cook for a minute.

Stir in the tomatoes, puree, Worcestershire sauce and stock and pour over the meat. Cover and cook in the oven for about 2½ hours or until the meat is tender.

Serve with creamy mashed potato to absorb the sauce. Serves 4.

Rösti

2 lb (900 g) large potatoes
½ level teaspoon salt
Freshly ground black pepper
2 oz (50 g) pork dripping

Scrub the potatoes and boil in salted water for 10 minutes or until the point of a knife can be inserted into the potato for about one inch (2.5 cm) before meeting resistance. Drain and cool and then peel and leave in a cool place overnight or chill for several hours.

Grate the potatoes coarsely into a bowl, add the seasoning and mix well.

Melt half the dripping in a non-stick frying pan and add the grated potato, flattening it with a fish slice. Cook very slowly over a low heat for 20 minutes, when the base will be golden brown. Turn out onto a large plate. Melt the remaining dripping in the pan and slide the potato cake off the plate and back into the pan to brown the second side, very slowly as before.

Turn onto a warm dish and serve. Serves 4-6.

Cook's Tip *Serve as an accompaniment to Veal Zurich or on its own for a tasty supper for the children topped with fried eggs.*

Swiss Salad

Even in the heart of winter the Swiss serve wonderful salads. They often include a mixture of sliced curly endive, broken leaves of a firm lettuce such as Iceberg, a few heads of Lambs lettuce or corn salad and some broken leaves of red chicory. This is all tossed just before serving in French dressing with some added herbs such as chopped basil.

Muesli

1 lb (450 g) Country muesli or
 1 lb (450 g) muesli base to include rolled oats, wheat flakes, rye flakes and barley flakes
2 oz (50 g) hazelnuts, chopped
2 oz (50 g) sultanas
2 oz (50 g) dates, chopped
2 oz (50 g) dried apricots, chopped
2 oz (50 g) dried apple, chopped
2 oz (50 g) sunflower seeds

Thoroughly mix all the ingredients together and then serve with milk or cream and a little demerara sugar.

Store in an airtight container.

Makes 1¾ lb (800 g) muesli. Use about 2 tablespoons to each serving.

Swiss Cherry Torte

4 eggs
4 oz (100 g) caster sugar
3 oz (75 g) self-raising flour
1 oz (25 g) cocoa

Filling:
15 oz (420 g) can black cherries, stoned
1 level tablespoon cornflour
2 tablespoons kirsch or
 6 tablespoons black cherry jam

Topping:
½ pint (300 ml) whipping cream, whipped
Chocolate curls or grated chocolate
A few fresh cherries

Swiss Cherry Torte

Heat the oven to 350 deg.F, 180 deg.C, gas mark 4. Grease and line with greased greaseproof paper two 9 inch (22.5 cm) sandwich tins.

Break the eggs into a mixing bowl, add sugar and either whisk with an electric whisk until thick enough for the whisk to leave a faint trail when lifted out of the bowl, or use a hand ballon whisk in a bowl standing over a pan of hot water. Fold in the sieved flour and cocoa, using a metal spoon. Divide carefully between the tins and bake for about 20 to 25 minutes until well risen and the sponges are beginning to shrink away from the sides of the tin. Turn onto a wire rack to cool.

Drain the can of cherries and save the juice.

Place the cornflour in a small saucepan and stir in the cherry juice over a moderate heat. Bring to the boil, stirring until thickened, simmer for 2 minutes and then remove from the heat and cool. Add the kirsch and cherries to the sauce. If using jam put in a bowl and stir in the kirsch before adding.

Sandwich the sponges together with a little whipped cream and cherry mixture keeping back some of the sauce for topping. Spread cream thinly around the sides of the cake. Coat with chocolate curls or grated chocolate. Spread the top with the reserved sauce and then pipe rosettes of cream all over.

Decorate with more chocolate curls or grated chocolate and a few fresh black cherries if available. Serves 10 to 12.

Glühwein

2 lemons
1 bottle inexpensive red wine
1 pint (600 ml) water
8 cloves
1 stick cinnamon
2-4 oz (50-100 g) caster sugar
4 tablespoons cheap brandy or sherry

Thinly peel the zest from the lemons. Cut a few slices for garnish and then squeeze the remaining fruit to extract all the juice.

Put the lemon zest, juice, wine, water, cloves and cinnamon in a saucepan. Put on the lid, bring the mixture to just below simmering point and leave at this temperature for an hour or more.

Remove the lemon rind, cloves and cinnamon and add sugar to taste. Add the brandy just before serving to get a more potent drink. Serve hot with slices of lemon floating on top. Serves 6.

CÔTES
BUZET
1973
FROMAGE
FABRIQUÉ EN
FABRIQUÉ AU LAIT CRU
FABRIQUÉ EN LAITERIE PAR LES Ets PIERRE
14290 - ORBEC EN AUGE
POIDS NET A L'EMBALLAGE
45 POUR CENT DE MATIÈRE GRASSE
MOULÉ A LA POCHE

FRANCE

In France a greater range of wines is produced than in any other country in the world and the food is as varied as the climate. Normandy and Brittany in the north are the lands of dairy farming and the kitchen garden, renowned for their cheeses and spring vegetables. Good fresh food is cooked simply in butter and often washed down with strong local cider. Richer dishes are to be found further south where olive oil replaces butter as the cooking medium and garlic and fresh herbs abound.

The Mediterranean and Atlantic coasts are famous for their shellfish, and the Perigord for its pâté: in fact everywhere in France local ingredients give to the cuisine their own distinctive flavours, and truly dedicated preparation creates a first-class standard of cooking.

French Onion Soup

2 oz (50 g) good dripping
1 lb (450 g) onions, finely chopped
1 oz (25 g) flour
1½ pints (900 ml) good beef stock
Salt and pepper
Gravy browning
2 oz (50 g) Cheddar cheese, grated

Melt the dripping in a large pan and add the onion and fry gently stirring occasionally until it begins to brown. Stir in the flour and cook stirring constantly until the mixture is browned. Gradually add the stock and bring to the boil, stirring all the time. Add the seasoning and a little gravy browning to give a good colour.

Cover the pan and simmer for 40 minutes, taste and check seasoning and serve hot sprinkled with the cheese. Serves 4.

1 Doux de montagne
2 Tomme au raisin
3 Roquefort
4 Walnut cheese
5 Boursin
6 Hazelnut cheese
7 Neufchâtel
8 Cheese with herbs
9 Brie
10 Port Salut
11 Chèvre
12 Bleu de Bresse
13 Camembert

Cheese Aigrettes

Serve as a savoury first course or as a snack with drinks.

1 oz (25 g) butter
¼ pint (150 ml) water
2 oz (50 g) self-raising flour
1 egg yolk
1 egg
2 oz (50 g) Cheddar cheese, grated
Salt
Cayenne pepper

Put the butter and water in a small saucepan and bring to the boil. Remove from the heat and add the flour, beating well until the mixture is glossy and leaves the sides of the pan clean. Cool slightly.

Lightly mix the yolk and the egg together and beat into the mixture a little at a time. Stir in the cheese, salt and a pinch of cayenne pepper. Check seasoning.

When required, drop the mixture in heaped teaspoonfuls into hot deep fat and fry gently until golden brown, turning once. Lift out and drain on kitchen paper. Serve at once.

French Country Pâté

12 oz (350 g) pigs' liver
1 small onion
8 oz (225 g) pork sausagemeat
½ level teaspoon salt
Freshly ground black pepper
1½ level tablespoons freshly chopped mixed herbs
1 clove garlic, crushed
1 egg
2 bayleaves
5 to 6 rashers streaky bacon

Cook's Tip *To check the seasoning in your pâté, take a spoonful of the mixture before it's ready to go into the dish and fry it gently in butter for about 5 minutes. Taste this sample and adjust seasoning.*

Heat the oven to 325 deg.F, 160 deg.C, gas mark 3.

Mince the liver and onion and put in a bowl with the sausagemeat, seasoning, herbs, garlic and egg and mix well.

Arrange the bayleaves in the bottom of a 1 lb (450 g) loaf tin. Remove the rind and any bone from the bacon, smooth with the back of a knife and use to line the loaf tin, making sure that the bayleaves stay in place.

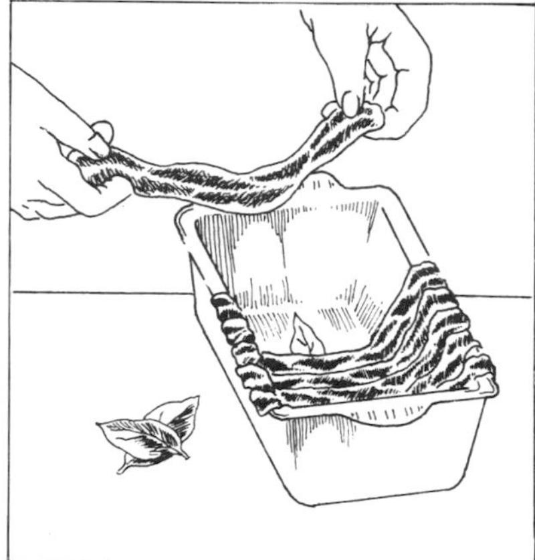

Press the meat mixture into the tin and smooth the top. Cover with a piece of foil. Place in a roasting tin half filled with hot water and cook for 1½ hours. The pâté is cooked when it has slightly shrunk from the sides of the tin and if the juices run clear when the centre is pierced with a skewer.

Remove from the oven and lightly weight the pâté with weights or tins. When quite cold chill in the refrigerator overnight. Turn out and serve sliced with chunks of hot French bread or toast. Serves 6 to 8.

Mediterranean Fish Casserole

Monk fish is inexpensive compared with the other firm fleshed fish like halibut and turbot.

1 lb (450 g) monk fish, skinned
1 oz (25 g) butter
8 oz (225 g) onion, chopped
1 fat clove garlic, crushed
14 oz (397 g) can peeled tomatoes
¼ pint (150 ml) dry vermouth
Sprig of lemon thyme
Salt and black pepper
Chopped parsley
Fresh prawns (optional)

Cut the fish into 1 inch (2.5 cm) cubes, removing any filmy tissue with a knife. Melt the butter in a large shallow pan. Add the onion and fry until almost tender, allowing it to become a pale golden. Add the garlic, tomatoes, vermouth, thyme and seasoning. Boil rapidly (without a lid) for 3 minutes to reduce it slightly. Add the fish and cook for a further 3 to 5 minutes until no longer transparent – it should be firm and white.

Remove the thyme, turn into a warm dish, scatter with chopped parsley and fresh prawns if liked.

Serve either with boiled rice or lots of garlic bread. Serves 4.

Moules Marinières

6 pints (3.4 l) fresh mussels
1 oz (25 g) butter
1 large onion, chopped
4 stalks parsley
2 sprigs fresh thyme
1 bayleaf
Freshly ground black pepper
½ pint (300 ml) dry white wine or cider
Salt
Chopped parsley

Beurre manié:
1 oz (25 g) creamed soft butter
½ oz (12.5 g) flour

Cook's Tip *Discard any mussels which are badly chipped or cracked or that do not close tightly. Those which remain open are dead and should not be used.*

Scrape and clean each mussel with a strong knife, removing every trace of seaweed, mud and beard. Wash in several changes of water. Drain in a colander.

Melt the butter in a large pan over a low heat. Add the onion to the pan and fry until soft but not coloured. Add the herbs, pepper, wine, salt and mussels, cover with a tightly fitting lid and cook quickly, shaking the pan constantly until the mussels open. This takes about 5 or 6 minutes. Lift the mussels out, discard the empty half of the shell and keep hot in a covered dish. Boil the cooking liquor to reduce to about ½ pint (300 ml), remove the herbs.

Moules Marinières

Blend the butter and flour together to a smooth paste. Drop into the simmering stock a teaspoonful at a time and whisk until the stock is smooth and has thickened. Taste and check seasoning and then pour over the mussels and sprinkle with plenty of chopped parsley.

Serve with French bread and butter. Finger bowls are a help, and you will need a dish for the empty shells. Serves 6.

Sole Florentine

This is an unusual recipe in that the fish is not cooked before the dish is assembled. Use fresh spinach if you have it.

4 large fillets of sole, skinned
Salt and ground black pepper

Juice of ½ a lemon
2 oz (50 g) butter
2 oz (50 g) flour
1 pint (600 ml) milk
1 lb (450 g) frozen leaf spinach (cooked as directed)
2 oz (50 g) grated Cheddar cheese
1 oz (25 g) fresh white breadcrumbs

Heat the oven to 400 deg.F, 200 deg.C, gas mark 6.

Season the fillets well with salt, pepper and lemon juice and roll up.

Melt the butter in a small saucepan, add the flour and cook for a minute. Stir in the milk and bring to the boil, stirring until thickened. Simmer for two minutes and season well. Blend six tablespoons of the sauce with the spinach and place in a 2 pint (a good litre) ovenproof dish.

Arrange the fish on top and spoon over the remaining sauce.

Mix the cheese and breadcrumbs together and sprinkle on top of the sauce. Bake in the oven for 20 minutes until the top is pale brown and the fish perfectly white. Serves 4.

Salade Niçoise

4 tomatoes
8 oz (225 g) French beans, cooked
1 crisp lettuce heart
⅛ pint (75 ml) French dressing (see page 00)
1 clove garlic, crushed
7 oz (200 g) can tuna fish
2 oz (50 g) can anchovy fillets
8 black olives
1 onion, finely sliced
2 hard-boiled eggs, quartered

Cook's Tip *Cos or Webb's lettuce are perfect for this. Don't use a flabby round lettuce as it doesn't have the crispness.*

Plunge the tomatoes in boiling water for a few minutes, then drain and skin, cut in quarters and remove all the seeds.

Cut the French beans into short even lengths.

Wash the lettuce and tear into strips and place in a salad bowl with the beans.

Flavour the French dressing with the garlic and add half to the salad bowl, tossing with the lettuce and beans.

Drain and flake the tuna and arrange with the drained anchovy fillets, olives and onion rings on top of the lettuce and beans.

Decorate the salad bowl with the quartered tomatoes and eggs and sprinkle over the remaining French dressing. Serves 4.

French Dressing

½ clove garlic, crushed
½ teaspoon dry mustard
½ teaspoon salt
Pinch freshly ground black pepper
1 level teaspoon caster sugar
¼ pint (150 ml) olive, corn or salad oil
4-6 tablespoons cider or white wine vinegar

Blend the first five ingredients together in a bowl and then gradually mix in the oil with a whisk or spoon.

Stir in the vinegar, taste and adjust seasoning if necessary. This makes ½ pint (300 ml) dressing.

Cook's Tip *Make in a quantity in the summer and keep in a cool larder or if warm in the refrigerator. Shake well before using. A good pinch of curry powder added to the recipe gives spice if you like it.*

Tossed Green Salad

2 lettuces
2 heads chicory
4 sticks celery, sliced
1 cucumber
Small green pepper
3 spring onions
1 avocado pear
About ⅛ pint (75 ml) French dressing
2 tablespoons sunflower seeds

Wash and drain the lettuce and break into small pieces. Slice the chicory or break into leaves and put in a large bowl with the celery. Skin the cucumber, cut in half lengthwise and then cut across into slices, add to the bowl. Remove the seeds and white pith from the pepper and cut into thin strips. Chop the spring onions. Peel the avocado pear, remove the stone and roughly chop.

Put the French dressing in a wooden salad bowl, add the avodado pear and toss until well coated.

Just before serving add all the other salad ingredients and toss well. Sprinkle with sunflower seeds. Serves 10 to 12.

Cook's Tip *Put French dressing in the serving bowl with any snipped chives, herbs or spring onion tops. Add the salad and toss well.*

Filet de Porc aux Pruneaux

(Fillet of pork with prune stuffing)

A rather special dish for a dinner party, it can be made in advance, kept in the refrigerator and then

just put in the oven to cook the pastry for the last 30 minutes. Serve with young carrots and mange tout if in season.

4 oz (100 g) prunes
1 onion, chopped
4 oz (100 g) streaky bacon, chopped
2 oz (50 g) fresh brown breadcrumbs
Salt and pepper
2 rounded tablespoons chopped parsley
2 pork fillets
1 oz (25 g) butter
1 tablespoon oil

Sauce:
Juices from the pork fillet
4 oz (100 g) mushrooms, chopped
1 oz (25 g) flour
½ pint (300 ml) dry cider
¼ pint (150 ml) chicken stock

14 oz (397 g) packet puff pastry
A little beaten egg

Cover the prunes with boiling water and leave to stand overnight. Next day, drain and remove all the stones and roughly chop.

Put the onion and bacon in a saucepan and fry over a moderate heat until the fat runs from the bacon. Stir in the prunes, breadcrumbs, seasoning and herbs.

Heat the oven to 400 deg.F, 200 deg.C, gas mark 6.

Carefully slice the fillets almost through to the other side lengthwise and open flat and season. Cover cut side with the stuffing and then cover with the other piece of fillet, cut side down onto the stuffing. Secure with fine string.

Place the fillets in a baking tin with the butter and oil and roast for 45 minutes or until pork fillet is cooked and the juices run clear, basting occasionally. Remove from oven, lift onto a plate and leave to cool.

Strain the juices from the roasting tin into a small saucepan. Add the mushrooms to the pan and cook gently for 5 minutes. Stir in the flour and cook for a minute. Add the cider and stock and bring to the boil, stirring. Simmer for two minutes, then taste and check seasoning and leave on one side until required to re-heat and serve with the pork.

Roll out the pastry to a square 12 inches (30 cm). Place the fillet in the centre and remove the string. Wrap the pastry over the fillet as you would a parcel, sealing the edges with a little beaten egg. Decorate the top with pastry leaves if liked and glaze all over with beaten egg.

Place on a baking tray and bake in the oven at 400 deg.F, 200 deg.C, gas mark 6 for 30 minutes until the pastry is well risen and golden brown. Serves 6.

Lamb Boulangère

Delicious with casseroled carrots cooked in the oven in butter and stock.

1 small leg of lamb
2 cloves garlic
Sprig of fresh rosemary
1½ lb (675 g) potatoes
8 oz (225 g) onions
Salt and pepper
½ pint (300 ml) stock
A little chopped parsley

Heat the oven to 375 deg.F, 190 deg.C, gas mark 5.

Trim any excess fat from the lamb and then peel the garlic, cut into thin slivers and insert into the lamb. Tie the sprig of rosemary over the lamb.

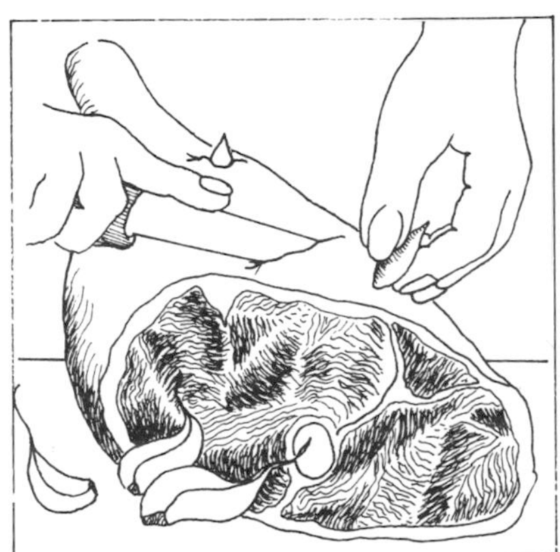

Peel the potatoes and cut into thick slices. Peel and thinly slice the onions, mix with the potatoes and then lay in a shallow

ovenproof dish and season well. Place the lamb on top and pour over the stock. Cover with a piece of foil and roast in the oven for 30 minutes to the lb (450 g) and 30 minutes over. After the first hour, remove the foil, baste the meat and vegetables and cook until tender.

When cooked, untie the rosemary and lay a fresh sprig in its place. Sprinkle the vegetables with a little chopped parsley. Serves 6 to 8.

French Beef Casserole

I often make double the quantity of this dish and use the rest as the filling for a pie.

1½ lb (675 g) chuck steak
½ pint (300 ml) red wine
2 tablespoons oil
Bayleaf
Ground black pepper
1 clove garlic, crushed
8 oz (225 g) onions, sliced
8 oz (225 g) carrots, sliced
6 oz (175 g) unsmoked streaky bacon
14 oz (397 g) can peeled tomatoes
Salt
4 oz (100 g) mushrooms, quartered

Cut the meat into 1 inch (2.5 cm) squares and put in a large china or glass bowl with the wine, oil, bayleaf, pepper, garlic, onions and carrots. Stir well then cover with a piece of cling film or foil and then leave in a cool place to marinate overnight.

Heat the oven to 300 deg.F, 150 deg.C, gas mark 2.

Remove the rind and any bone from the bacon and cut into strips. Put half in a 4 pint (2.3 l) ovenproof dish, then put the meat and marinade on top and cover with the remaining bacon and can of tomatoes. Season with salt and then cover the dish and cook in the oven for 3 hours. Stir in the mushrooms and cook for a further 15 to 30 minutes or until the beef is tender.

Taste and check seasoning and remove the bayleaf. Serves 6.

Chicken Marengo

Traditionally this dish is served garnished with fried eggs and croûtons of fried bread. In England we leave out the eggs and just garnish with the croûtons.

2 tablespoons oil
1 oz (25 g) butter
6 chicken joints
1 oz (25 g) flour
½ pint (300 ml) dry white wine
¼ pint (150 ml) chicken stock
14 oz (397 g) can tomatoes
Salt and pepper
1 clove garlic, crushed
6 oz (175 g) button mushrooms
Croûtons of fried bread

Heat the oil and butter in a large frying pan and fry the chicken quickly until brown on both sides. Lift out and put on a plate. Add the flour to the pan and cook for a minute or two, stir in the wine and stock and bring to the boil, stirring until thickened. Add tomatoes, seasoning and garlic and then return the chicken to the pan. Cover and simmer for 30 minutes. Then add the mushrooms left whole and continue cooking for a further 15 minutes or until the chicken is tender. Taste and check seasoning, arrange the chicken on a warm serving dish and spoon the sauce over.

Garnish with the croûtons of fried bread. Serves 6.

Chicken Marengo

French Cheeseboard

In France, the cheeseboard is usually served between the main course and the dessert. This is practical, as you can continue enjoying a red wine with the cheese and finish with something sweet. Take a tip from the French and take care with presentation. Choose a selection of cheeses, hard, soft and blue. Cover your board with vine leaves if you have them or if not, the leaves from any attractive fruit tree or bush, such as blackcurrant. A bunch of grapes or a pile of cherries on the board look appetising too.

Keep cheeses loosely wrapped in cling film in the fridge and take out ½ hour before needed.

Crêpes Suzette

8 to 10 pancakes (see page 11)

Sauce:
Juice of 2 oranges
4 oz (100 g) unsalted butter
2 oz (50 g) caster sugar
1 tablespoon orange liqueur
3 tablespoons brandy

Put the orange juice, butter and sugar in a large frying pan and heat gently until the sugar has dissolved. Simmer for about 5 minutes until the sauce is syrupy.

Lay one pancake in the pan and coat with the sauce. Fold in four (to make a triangle) and move to one side of the pan. Repeat with the remaining pancakes. Making sure that the pancakes are piping hot, add the liqueur and brandy. If you wish, light with a match, then arrange on a serving dish and serve at once. Serves 4 to 5.

Cook's Tip *If you don't have a large enough frying pan, remove the pancakes that you have cooked and keep hot on one side.*

Fresh Apricot and Almond Tart

Pastry:
6 oz (175 g) plain flour
4 oz (100 g) butter
1 egg yolk
Level tablespoon caster sugar
2 teaspoons cold water

Crème patissière:
3 egg yolks
3 oz (75 g) vanilla sugar or use caster sugar and ½ teaspoon vanilla essence
1 oz (25 g) flour
½ pint (300 ml) milk

Topping:
1½ lb (675 g) apricots
Juice of ½ lemon
6 tablespoons water
2 oz (50 g) caster sugar
Scant teaspoon arrowroot
1 tablespoon brandy
½ oz (12.5 g) toasted flaked almonds

First make the pastry: Put the flour in a bowl, add fat cut in small pieces and rub in with the fingertips until the mixture resembles fine breadcrumbs.

Mix the egg yolk, sugar and water, stir into the dry ingredients and bind them together. Roll out the pastry on a floured table, line a 9 inch (22.5 cm) flan tin and chill for 30 minutes.

Heat the oven to 435 deg.F, 225 deg.C, gas mark 7 with a thick baking sheet in it. Line the flan with greaseproof paper and baking beans and bake blind for 10 minutes or until beginning to brown at the edges. Remove the paper and beans and return to the oven for a further 5 minutes to cook the centre through. Cool in the tin and then carefully lift onto a serving plate.

To make the crème patissière: Put egg yolks, sugar and flour in a bowl with a little milk and mix to a smooth mixture with a wire whisk. Boil the rest of the milk and pour onto the yolks, whisking well. Rinse out the pan, then return the mixture to the pan and stir over a low heat until thickened. Remove from the heat and leave to cool, stirring occasionally. Spread in the flan case.

Wash the apricots, halve and remove stones. Put lemon juice and water in a large shallow pan. Add apricots cut side down and sprinkle with sugar, then cover with a tight-fitting lid.

Bring to the boil, then simmer very gently for about 5 minutes until the fruit is just soft. Lift out with a slotted spoon and place on top of the crème patissière. Measure the arrowroot into a bowl and mix with brandy, then

Fresh Apricot and Almond Tart

with the juices in the pan. Return to the pan, bring to the boil and allow to thicken. If it seems too thick to coat the fruit, thin down with a little water. Add the almonds to the glaze then spoon over the tart to give a shiny top. Serves 6 to 8.

Mousse au Citron

2 large lemons
½ oz (12.5 g) gelatine
3 tablespoons water
3 eggs, separated
3-4 oz (75-100 g) caster sugar or to taste
¼ pint (150 ml) double cream, whipped

Finely grate the rind and squeeze the juice from the lemons. Place the gelatine and water in a small bowl or cup. Stand for 3 minutes until it becomes spongy, then stand bowl in a pan of simmering water and let the gelatine dissolve. Keep warm.

Put the egg yolks, lemon juice and rind with the sugar in a large bowl, stand over a pan of simmering water and whisk until thick and creamy: this will take about 10 minutes. Remove from the heat and continue whisking until cool, then pour in the gelatine, whisking all the time until well blended.

Whisk the egg whites with an electric or hand rotary whisk until fairly stiff, then fold in first the cream then the lemon mixture until everything is smoothly blended

Pour into a 2½ pint (1.4 l) dish, smooth the top and leave in a cool place to set. Serves 6.

Raspberry and Strawberry Brûlée

8 oz (225 g) strawberries
8 oz (225 g) raspberries
About 2 oz (50 g) icing sugar
3-4 tablespoons brandy
½ pint (300 ml) double cream
Light soft brown sugar

Hull the strawberries and if very large cut in half. Place in a bowl with the raspberries and sprinkle with icing sugar. Cover and chill thoroughly for several hours.

Divide the mixture between six individual overproof dishes or fill one large ovenproof dish, capacity about 2½ pints (1.4 l). Leave plenty of room for the cream to bubble up in the cooking.

Sprinkle the brandy over the fruit. Lightly whip the cream until it just forms soft peaks and spread over the top of the fruit. Scatter the sugar quite thickly, but at random, over the top of the cream so that not all the surface is covered. Put under a hot grill until the sugar goes a deep golden brown. Serve at once. Serves 6-8.

Chocolate Eclairs

Chocolate Éclairs

Choux pastry:
2 oz (50 g) butter
¼ pint (150 ml) water
2½ oz (62 g) plain flour
2 eggs, beaten

Filling:
½ pint (300 ml) whipping cream

Icing:
1½ oz (40 g) butter
1 oz (25 g) cocoa
4 oz (100 g) icing sugar, sieved
3-4 tablespoons milk

Heat the oven to 425 deg.F, 220 deg.C, gas mark 7. Grease two baking trays.

Put the butter and water in a small pan and bring to the boil slowly to allow the butter to melt. Remove from the heat, add the flour all at once and beat to form a ball. Gradually beat in the eggs a little at a time to make a smooth paste.

Put the mixture into a piping bag fitted with a ½ inch (1.25 cm) pipe and pipe the mixture into 4 inch (8 cm) lengths on the baking trays. It will make about 14 éclairs.

Bake in the oven for 10 minutes then reduce the heat to 375 deg.F, 190 deg.C, gas mark 5 and cook for a further 15 to 20 minutes until golden brown, risen and crisp.

Remove from the oven and slit down one side of each éclair to allow the steam to escape, leave to cool on a wire rack.

Whip the cream until it is thick and forms peaks and fill the éclairs.

Make the icing: Melt the butter in a small saucepan, add cocoa and cook for a minute. Remove from the heat and stir in the icing sugar and milk, beat well until starting to thicken and then coat over each éclair.

Leave to set and serve on the same day that they are made. Makes 14 éclairs.

ITALY

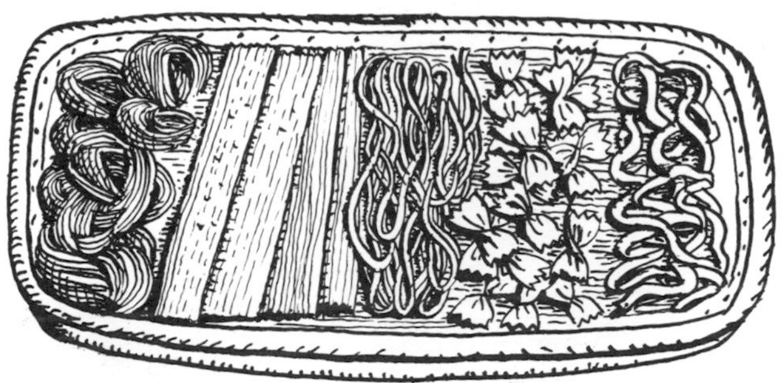

The cuisine and the wines of Italy are amongst the finest in the world. Spaghetti is certainly an extremely popular dish, but there are many other different types of pasta and an equal variety of sauces to go with it. A number of sauces are based on olive oil, tomatoes and garlic; they may contain cheese, fish, herbs or, as in the case of the Bolognese, meat. Pasta, whether in minestrone or lasagne, or simply in a cream sauce with garlic, is usually eaten as a first course, and a healthy appetite is needed to follow it up with a main dish of veal, fish or chicken, often served in a rich cream sauce. Soups and pasta are garnished with grated Parmesan and the meal is rounded off with one of Italy's famous cheeses, such as Dolcelatte, Bel Paese or Ricotta, fresh fruit or a light dessert like ice cream or Zabaglione.

Minestrone

1 oz (25 g) bacon fat
1 large onion, finely chopped
3 carrots, finely diced
2 sticks celery, finely chopped
1 leek, thinly sliced
2½ pints (1.4 l) beef or chicken stock
2 level tablespoons tomato puree
1 level teaspoon salt
Black pepper to taste
3 oz (75 g) spaghetti broken into 1½ inch (3.75 cm) lengths
¼ small cabbage, finely shredded

Cook's Tip *A good main meal soup. Sprinkle with Parmesan cheese if liked and serve hot with brown rolls and butter.*

If making your own stock, strip any pieces of meat from the bones and chop them up. Put on one side to add to the soup.

Melt the bacon fat in a saucepan and fry the onion until it begins to colour. Add the carrots, celery and leek and fry gently for 8-10 minutes, stirring frequently. Add the stock, tomato puree, salt and pepper and bring to the boil. Cover and simmer for 30 minutes until all the vegetables are tender. Add any chicken meat or small pieces of beef with the spaghetti and cabbage and cook for a further 10 minutes, stirring occasionally.

Taste and check seasoning. Serves 6.

Risotto Milanese

2 oz (50 g) butter
1 small onion, chopped
8 oz (225 g) long grain rice
¼ pint (150 ml) dry white wine
1 pint (600 ml) chicken stock
Salt and pepper
A good pinch powdered saffron
2 teaspoons water
1 oz (25 g) Parmesan cheese, grated

Cook's Tip *If you can't find saffron, add a teaspoon of powdered turmeric to the stock when cooking the rice.*

Melt 1 oz (25 g) butter in a saucepan and fry the onion over a low heat until soft, but not brown. Add the rice to the pan and continue to cook it for 2 minutes. Pour on the wine and simmer for a few minutes. Add the stock with lots of salt and pepper. Bring to the boil, cover the saucepan and let the risotto simmer for about 20 minutes or until the rice is tender and all the liquid has been absorbed.

Blend the saffron with the water and stir into the rice, using a fork. Then add the remaining butter and cheese, taste and check seasoning and then serve on a hot dish. Serves 4.

Osso Buco

Cook's Tip *A rich Italian stew, ideally made from knuckle of veal, with the marrow in the bone carefully preserved. If you have difficulty in getting knuckle use pie veal.*

About 4 lb (2 kg) knuckle veal or 1½ lb (675 g) pie veal
1 tablespoon oil
½ oz (12.5 g) butter
3 carrots, peeled and sliced
2 sticks celery, sliced
1 onion, chopped
1 large fat clove garlic, crushed
½ oz (12.5 g) flour
¼ pint (150 ml) dry white wine
¼ pint (150 ml) chicken stock
14 oz (397 g) can peeled tomatoes

Osso Buco accompanied by Risotto Milanese

1974
Barolo
riserva

1 sprig parsley
1 bayleaf
Salt and pepper

Garnish:
Grated rind of ½ lemon
2 tablespoons chopped parsley and basil

Heat oven to 325 deg.F, 160 deg.C, gas mark 3.

Ask the butcher to saw the knuckle into 2 inch (5 cm) sized chunks, or if using pie veal cut into 1½ inch (3.75 cm) pieces.

Heat the oil and butter in a large frying pan and fry the meat, half at a time, over a moderate heat, turning once to brown. Lift out with a slotted spoon and place in a large casserole.

Add the vegetables to the pan and fry lightly for 5 minutes. Stir in the flour, then add the wine and stock, tomatoes, parsley, bayleaf, salt and pepper. Bring to the boil and then pour over the meat.

Cover with a lid, put into the oven and cook for about 2½ hours or until the veal is tender.

For the garnish mix together the lemon rind, parsley and basil and when serving the casserole, sprinkle on top. Serves 4.

Spaghetti Bolognese

2 tablespoons oil
8 oz (225 g) onions, chopped
2 sticks celery, sliced
1 lb (450 g) good minced beef
1 good oz (25 g) flour
2 cloves garlic, crushed
2½ oz (62 g) can tomato puree
¼ pint (150 ml) beef stock
¼ pint (150 ml) red wine
14 oz (397 g) can peeled tomatoes
1 tablespoon redcurrant jelly
1 level teaspoon salt
Freshly ground black pepper
12 oz (350 g) spaghetti
Parmesan cheese

Heat the oil in a pan and fry the onions, celery and beef for 5 minutes. Stir in the flour, garlic and tomato puree and cook for a minute. Add the stock, wine, tomatoes, redcurrant jelly and seasoning and bring to the boil, stirring until thickened. Reduce the heat, partially cover the pan and simmer gently for one hour.

Cook the spaghetti in a pan of fast boiling salted water (about two teaspoons salt to every four pints water) until tender. When ready the spaghetti should be slightly firm to bite but not hard in the centre.

Strain through a colander and rinse out the saucepan. Add a little oil or a large knob of butter, return the pasta to the pan and toss gently.

Serve the spaghetti onto plates and ladle the sauce on top. Hand the Parmesan cheese separately. Serves 4 to 6.

Tagliatelle with Garlic Cream Sauce

8 oz (225 g) tagliatelle
A good knob of butter
Large clove garlic, crushed
¼ pint (150 ml) double cream
1 rounded tablespoon chopped parsley
Salt and freshly ground black pepper

Cook the tagliatelle in plenty of fast boiling salted water until just soft as directed on the packet. Drain very well and rinse in warm water and then drain again.

Rinse out the saucepan, melt the butter, add the garlic and fry for 2-3 minutes. Stir the cream into the pan with the parsley and then add the tagliatelle and toss well until coated with the sauce. Taste and add salt and plenty of ground black pepper. Turn into a warm dish and serve. Serves 4 for a first course.

Lasagne

5 oz (150 g) uncooked lasagne

Meat Sauce:
1 tablespoon oil
1 lb (450 g) minced beef
1 oz (25 g) streaky bacon, derinded and chopped
8 oz (225 g) onion, chopped
4 sticks celery, chopped
½ oz (12.5 g) flour
½ pint (300 ml) water
3½ oz (90 g) can tomato puree
2 cloves garlic, crushed
2 teaspoons brown sugar
1 beef stock cube
½ teaspoon salt
Pepper
¼ teaspoon mixed dried herbs

White sauce:
1½ oz (40 g) butter
1½ oz (40 g) flour
¼ teaspoon nutmeg
Salt and pepper
1 pint (600 ml) milk
½ teaspoon made mustard
4 oz (100 g) Cheddar cheese, grated
4 oz (100 g) Emmenthal cheese,

Tagliatelli with Garlic Cream Sauce

grated
½ oz (12.5 g) Parmesan cheese, grated

Cook's Tip *Save time by using this recipe for lasagne. There is no need to cook the pasta first.*

For the meat sauce: Heat oil in a pan, add the beef and bacon and fry until browned. Add onions and celery and cook for 5 minutes. Stir in the flour and remaining meat sauce ingredients, stir well and bring to the boil. Cover and simmer for an hour.

For the white sauce: Melt the butter in a large pan, stir in the flour, nutmeg, salt and pepper and cook gently for 2 minutes. Remove the pan from the heat, stir in the milk. Return the pan to the heat and bring to the boil, stirring until thickened. Add mustard and check seasoning.

Combine Cheddar and Emmenthal. In a shallow 3½ pint (2 l) ovenproof dish put a third of the meat sauce, the white sauce and a third of the cheese, followed by half of the uncooked lasagne (lay edge to edge, not overlapping). Then start again with a third of the meat sauce, white sauce and cheese and last half of the lasagne. Repeat, finishing with a final layer of meat sauce, white sauce and cheese and the grated Parmesan. Leave to become cold, then cook at 350 deg.F, 180 deg.C, gas mark 4 for about 45 minutes to an hour or until the top is golden brown and bubbling.

Serve at once or keep hot at 200 deg.F, 100 deg.C, gas mark ¼ for up to one hour if necessary. Serves 6.

Zabaglione

6 tablespoons marsala or Madeira
4 oz (100 g) caster sugar
4 egg yolks

Cook's Tip *Such a simple recipe. It can be made with whole eggs, which gives a very light texture, but is not so firm. If you have neither marsala nor Madeira use sweet sherry.*

Stand an oven glass bowl over a pan of simmering water. Measure the wine and sugar into the bowl,

leave to get really warm but not hot. Add the yolks and at once begin whisking and continue whisking until light and foamy. Pour into four large stemmed glasses, preferably with a wide brim.

Serve at once with thin sweet biscuits such as langue de chat. Serve 4.

Cassata

A beautiful looking traditional Italian ice cream. The preparation takes some time but the results will be well worth the trouble.

2 oz (50 g) mixed cherries, raisins, angelica and dried apricots, finely chopped
2 tablespoons brandy
4 eggs, separated
4 oz (100 g) caster sugar
½ pint (300 ml) double cream
¼ pint (150 ml) raspberry puree
About 2 tablespoons coffee essence or to taste

Put the finely chopped fruit in a small bowl with the brandy, cover and leave to stand overnight.

Whisk the yolks in a small bowl until blended. In a larger bowl whisk the egg whites with a hand rotary or electric whisk on high speed until stiff then whisk in the sugar a teaspoonful at a time; the egg whites will get stiffer and stiffer as the sugar is added.

Whisk the cream until it forms soft peaks and then fold into the meringue mixture with the egg yolks.

Divide the ice cream into three portions of varying size. To the largest portion add the raspberry puree and fold in until thoroughly mixed. Flavour the middle portion with coffee essence to give a good flavour and colour. Finely mix the soaked fruit into the smallest quantity of ice cream.

Put all the bowls in the deep freeze for 30 minutes. Take a 2¼ pint (1.3 l) toughened glass bowl and chill in the freezer with the ice cream.

Take out the bowl and the raspberry ice cream and use this to evenly coat the base and sides of the bowl to within one inch (2.5 cm) of the rim. Return to the freezer for 30 minutes. Then take out with the coffee ice cream and spread this over the raspberry ice cream. Return to the freezer for a further 30 minutes.

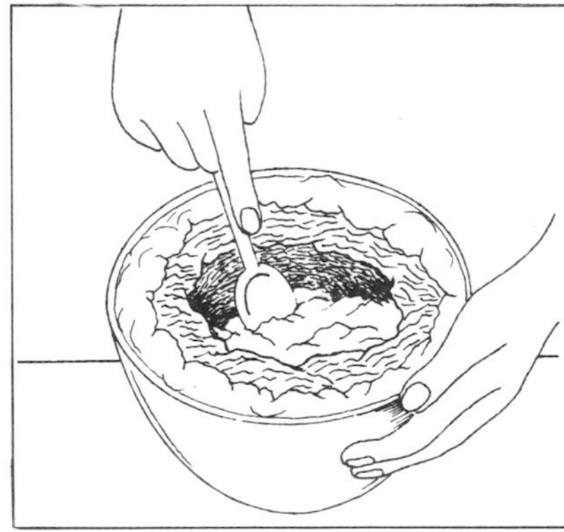

Remove the tutti frutti ice cream and stir lightly to mix, then put into the centre of the bowl, cover and return to the freezer. Chill for several hours.

To serve: Remove from the freezer and leave to stand at room temperature for 10 minutes. Wipe the bowl with a warm cloth and then run a knife around the bowl and turn out onto a plate. Serve cut in wedges. Serves 8 to 10.

PRODUCE OF GREECE
"ACHAIA"
CLAUSS
ACHAIA-CLAUSS
ALC 12% BY VOL

GREECE

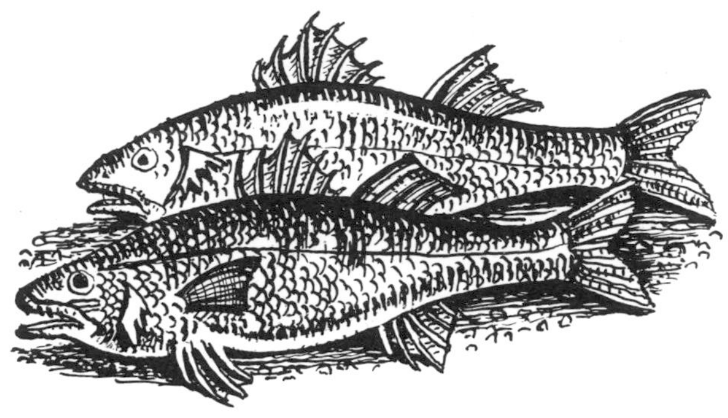

Greece is a land of wine and olives, fruit and fish, all of which go to make up a delicious and different cuisine. Vegetables such as tomatoes, aubergines, peppers, onions, potatoes and cauliflower grow abundantly. Lemon juice and olive oil are as essential to Greek cooking as is the grape of which every part is used. Vine twigs give an unmistakeable fragrance to barbequed meat or fish and the leaves are eaten filled with a savoury stuffing. If you haven't got a vine growing at home, vine leaves are available, marinated and sold in packets, from many large supermarkets. Lamb is the meat most frequently found in Greece, and it is often eaten minced in a combined dish with other foods. They are also known for Feta, a salty goats' cheese, and for their sweet pastries and syrupy sticky cakes.

Taramasalata

A pretty pink spread that makes a delightful summer starter.

8 oz (225 g) smoked cod's roe (can be bought in a jar)
2 small slices white bread, with crusts removed
2 tablespoons milk
1 clove garlic, crushed (optional)
¼ pint (150 ml) less 2 tablespoons oil
2 tablespoons lemon juice
Salt and pepper
2 bayleaves to garnish

Remove the skin from the cod's roe. Reduce to a paste in a blender or processor or place in a mortar and pound it with a pestle until smooth.

Soak the bread in the milk, then squeeze out as much milk as possible. Add the bread to the roe and blend or mash again with the garlic, if used. Add the oil one teaspoon at a time until all has been absorbed. Stir in the lemon juice and seasoning.

Turn into a small dish and chill well. When ready to serve, garnish the dish with bayleaves. Serve with hot buttered toast. Serves 4.

Feta Cheese Salad, Taramasalata and Hummus

Feta Cheese Salad

Feta is a pure white soft crumbly cheese. It is fairly salty and is the most popular cheese of Greece.

2 oz (50 g) fat black olives
½ crisp lettuce
½ cucumber, thickly sliced
½ green pepper, cubed
5 tablespoons French dressing (see page 29) made with olive oil
4 oz (100 g) Feta cheese
A tablespoon chopped fresh marjoram and parsley

Arrange the salad on individual plates. Cut the Feta cheese in triangles, then put with the salad.

Spoon over the dressing and sprinkle with herbs. Serves 4.

Hummus

This is delicious eaten with warm pitta bread

8 oz (225 g) dried chick peas
1½ teaspoons salt
3 cloves garlic, crushed
6 tablespoons lemon juice
5 oz (125 g) tahina paste
Cayenne pepper

Put the peas in a bowl after rinsing them, cover with cold water and leave to soak for at least 12 hours.

Drain the peas and put them in a saucepan. Add the salt and enough water to cover them, bring to the boil and simmer for 2-3 hours until they are very tender. Drain the peas and reserve the cooking water.

Mash the peas to a smooth puree with the garlic and 6 tablespoons of the cooking water (or use a blender). Add the lemon juice a little at a time, beating continually with a large spoon. Add the tahina paste, and beat until smooth.

Turn into a bowl and sprinkle with cayenne pepper. Serves 4.

Moussaka

About 1 lb (450 g) minced lamb
½ lb (225 g) onions, chopped
2 cloves garlic, crushed
1½ oz (40 g) flour
Salt and pepper
1 level teaspoon coriander seeds,

crushed
A little fresh or dried thyme
14 oz (397 g) can tomatoes
4 aubergines

Cook's Tip *In this recipe the aubergines are blanched in water instead of being fried. This makes the dish healthier and less heavy.*

Sauce:
1½ oz (40 g) butter
1½ oz (40 g) flour
¾ pint (450 ml) milk
1 level teaspoon made English mustard
Grated nutmeg
Salt and pepper
6 oz (75 g) Cheddar cheese, grated
1 egg, beaten
Chopped parsley

Heat the oven to 375 deg.F, 190 deg.C, gas mark 5. Butter a large ovenproof dish.

Turn the minced lamb into a large pan, cook over a low heat at first to let the fat run out of the meat and stir to avoid sticking. When the fat has run freely from the meat add the onions and garlic and increase the heat. Fry to brown the meat for about 15 minutes. If there seems to be an excess of fat, spoon off the surplus. Add flour, stir well, then add salt, pepper, coriander, thyme and the contents of the can of tomatoes. Bring to the boil and simmer for 5 minutes. Check seasoning.

Slice the aubergines and blanch in a pan of boiling water for 1 minute. This softens the skin and prevents the aubergines discolouring. Drain, then dry on kitchen paper.

Make the sauce by slowly melting the butter in a pan, add the flour and cook together for a few minutes over a medium heat without colouring. Blend in the milk, slowly at first, and bring to the boil, stirring well. Add mustard, nutmeg, salt, pepper and cheese. Cook to let the cheese melt, then remove from the heat. Cool slightly, then add the egg and mix well.

Now assemble the moussaka. First put a layer of half the meat mixture in the dish, cover with half the aubergines, season, then repeat with the rest of the lamb and aubergines, so that you end up with 4 layers. Pour over the cheese sauce.

Bake uncovered for 45 minutes to an hour until golden brown. Sprinkle with chopped parsley and serve hot. Serves 6-8.

Kleftico

A leg of lamb or a lean shoulder
4 cloves garlic, cut in spikes
Tablespoon rosemary or oregano
Juice of ½ lemon
Salt
Ground black pepper
Chopped parsley

Heat the oven to 425 deg.F, 220 deg.C, gas mark 7.

Make incisions into the lamb with a sharp pointed knife and in each hole slip a spike of garlic. Put the lamb in a roasting tin or casserole with herbs, lemon juice and seasoning.

Roast in the oven for 30 minutes to brown, then lower the heat to 275 deg.F, 140 deg.C, gas mark 1. Cover the dish and cook for a further 3½ hours until really tender so that when carved the meat falls off the bone. Take all the fat from the juices in the tin. Taste and check seasoning and serve the juices with the lamb.

Carve the lamb and scatter each portion with parsley. Serve with green beans and tomato sauce (see below) and small potatoes. First blanch the potatoes in boiling water for a minute and cook in oil and garlic under the meat for at least an hour. Serve scattered with chopped chives. Serves 8.

Green Beans in Tomato Sauce

2 lb (900 g) French beans
1 tablespoon oil
1 onion, finely chopped
1 large clove garlic, crushed
14 oz (397 g) can peeled tomatoes
½ teaspoon salt
Freshly ground black pepper
½ teaspoon sugar

Cook's Tip *This is a classic way of serving beans in Greece. I prefer to cook the whole beans in boiling salted water until al dente – just tender, then serve them with the sauce.*

Remove the ends from the beans. Place in a pan of boiling salted water, bring back to the boil and boil for one minute. Drain and put in an ovenproof dish.

Heat the oven to 275 deg.F, 140 deg.C, gas mark 1.

Heat the oil in a saucepan and add the onion, garlic and tomatoes and simmer with the lid off until reduced to a thick consistency. Add all the sea-

Kleftico, Green Beans in Tomato Sauce and Potatoes

sonings and pour over the beans. Cook in the oven for one hour. Serves 8.

Stuffed Vine Leaves

1 onion, chopped
1 lb (450 g) minced beef
3 oz (75 g) cooked long grain rice
1 level teaspoon salt
Ground black pepper
¼ pint (150 ml) beef stock
12-14 large vine leaves

Sauce:
1 oz (25 g) butter
1 oz (25 g) flour
¼ pint (150 ml) stock
14 oz (397 g) can peeled tomatoes
Bayleaf
¼ teaspoon mixed dried herbs
Salt and pepper

Cook's Tip *Cabbage leaves may be used if vine leaves are unobtainable, but they should be blanched for about 2 minutes and the hard stalk cut out.*

Place the onion and beef in a frying pan and gently fry for 5 minutes to allow the fat to run out. Skim off any excess fat and then stir in the rice, seasoning and stock and cook gently for about 20 minutes or until all the stock has been absorbed.

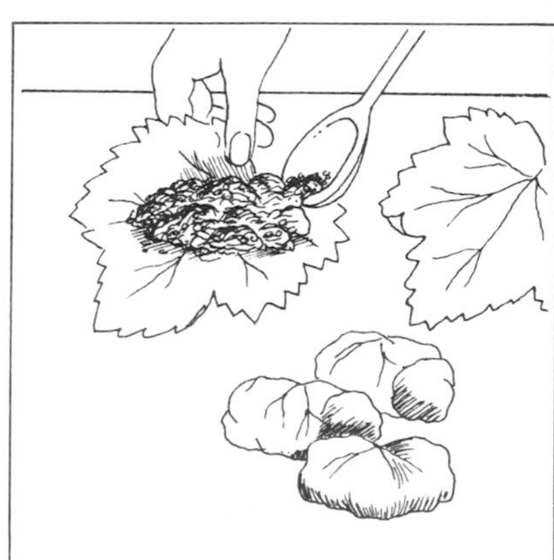

Cook the vine leaves in boiling water for a minute and drain well. Cut off the stalk and lay flat on a work surface.

For the sauce: Melt the butter in a saucepan, stir in the flour and add the stock and tomatoes with the bayleaf, herbs and seasoning and simmer for 20 minutes.

Baklava

Heat the oven to 350 deg.F, 180 deg.C, gas mark 4.

Place a spoonful of the meat mixture in the centre of each leaf, fold in the sides and roll up like a small parcel. Lay in a single layer in an ovenproof dish. Strain over the sauce and bake in the oven for 35-40 minutes.

If liked these may be served with a bowl of natural yoghurt. Serves 4 to 6.

Baklava

8 oz (225 g) phyllo pastry (also filo or fillo)
4 oz (100 g) unsalted butter, melted
4 oz (100 g) walnuts, chopped fairly finely
1 oz (25 g) caster sugar

Lemon syrup:
¼ pint (150 ml) water
8 oz (225 g) caster sugar
Thinly peeled rind and juice of 1 lemon

Heat the oven to 400 deg.F, 200 deg.C, gas mark 6. Butter a Swiss roll tin 11 by 7 inches (27.5 by 17.5 cm).

Cut the phyllo pastry in half so that it is roughly the size of the tin. Lay one sheet of pastry in the tin, brush with butter and continue until there are 8 layers in the tin. Brush the top layer with butter and sprinkle with nuts and sugar. Finish with a further 8 layers of pastry, brushing with butter between the layers. Brush the top with more butter and cut through to the tin into diamond shapes.

Bake for about 25 to 30 minutes until a pale golden brown and crispy. Cool.

Meanwhile make the lemon syrup. Put the water into a pan, add the sugar and the thinly peeled zest of the lemon, bring to the boil slowly and simmer for 15 minutes without a lid. Remove from the heat and add the lemon juice. Pour over the cold baklava or cool the syrup and pour over hot baklava.

Serve with whipped cream. Serves 8.

Galatopoureko

Make as for baklava (above) and put in a slightly bigger tin, but fill the centre – i.e. when 8 layers are reached – with crème patissière (see apricot tart page 32). Add 1 oz (25 g) sugar to the crème before cooling a little to spread. Top with a further 8 layers of pastry. Cut into squares through the top 4 layers with scissors and a sharp knife. Bake as for baklava but for 35 minutes until pale brown and crisp. Serve warm dusted with icing sugar and cut in squares.

AMERICA

The pioneering spirit of the Americans is as evident in their cooking as it is in their history. American cooking owes its great variety to the country's huge natural resources and a vast number of first and second generation ethnic groups who combine the traditions of the old country with the produce of the new. Americans are famous for their cookouts – in summer they hardly ever bother to cook indoors, preferring to cook hamburgers, meat and fish on a barbeque outside. American steaks are legendary, and often eaten on the same platter as a large helping of seafood. Thanksgiving is the high spot in the culinary year. Turkey is eaten with roast sweet potatoes and squash (vegetable marrow).

Corn Chowder

A quick soup to make and deliciously different.

5 rashers streaky bacon
1 oz (25 g) butter
1 large onion, sliced
12 oz (340 g) can corn niblets, drained
8 oz (225 g) cooked potato, finely diced
10.2 oz (290 g) can mushroom soup
1 pint (600 ml) milk
1 level teaspoon salt
Freshly ground black pepper

Remove the rind and bone from the bacon and cut into strips, place in a large saucepan with the butter and fry gently until the fat has run out and the bacon is golden brown and crisp. Lift out with a slotted spoon and put on one side.

Add the onion to the fat remaining in the pan and fry gently for 5 to 10 minutes until soft but not brown. Add the rest of the ingredients to the saucepan and bring to the boil, stirring, then reduce the heat and simmer for 10 minutes.

Taste and check seasoning and serve in bowls with the bacon sprinkled on top. Serves 6 to 8.

Avocado Mousse, Thanksgiving Turkey and Virginia Baked Ham

Avocado Mousse

A splendid first course to serve at a special dinner or luncheon.

½ oz (12.5 g) gelatine
4 tablespoons cold water
¼ pint (150 ml) boiling water
1 chicken stock cube
2 large avocado pears
1 level teaspoon salt
½ level teaspoon ground black pepper
Piece of onion the size of a walnut, crushed in a garlic press
1 tablespoon lemon juice
½ pint (300 ml) mayonnaise
¼ pint (150 ml) double cream, lightly whipped
Prawns for decoration

Place the gelatine and cold water in a small bowl. Stand for 3 minutes until consistency is spongy, then stand the bowl in a pan of simmering water and allow the gelatine to dissolve. Stir the boiling water and stock cube together until the cube has dissolved and stir in the gelatine.

Peel and quarter the avocados, removing the stones, and crush with a fork or potato masher, stir in stock, salt, pepper and onion and lemon juice. Alternatively, process in a blender. Leave to become quite cold and then fold in the mayonnaise and cream.

Pour into a 2 pint (a good litre) ring mould and leave in the refrigerator to set. Turn out and decorate with prawns. Serves 4 for lunch or 6 as a starter.

Virginia Baked Ham

5-6 lb (2.3-2.7 kg) piece of middle gammon, either on or off the bone as preferred
2 pints (1.1 l) cider
4 oz (100 g) brown sugar

Cook's Tip *I usually find it a good idea to soak the joint overnight to remove any excess saltiness. Ask advice from your butcher, he may suggest a longer soaking period.*

Glaze:
1 teaspoon dry mustard
About 2 oz (50 g) demerara sugar
A little of the cider stock

Decoration:
A few whole cranberries and half slices of canned pineapple

Soak the gammon overnight in cold water, then throw away the water. Put the joint in a pan just large enough to take it and pour over the cider, topping up with water if necessary to cover the joint. Put on the lid, bring to the boil and simmer for 1½ hours very gently. Then bring to a full rolling boil and at once lift pan onto a thick folded newspaper, then wrap completely in an old thick blanket or sleeping bag and leave for at least 6 hours to continue cooking in a hay box fashion.

Lift out the ham, carefully remove the skin and score the fat with a sharp knife as your would the skin of pork.

To glaze: Measure the mustard into a small bowl, add the sugar and mix to a thin paste with some of the cider stock. Spread over the fat, cover the lean meat with foil and brown the fatty skin in a hot oven at 425 deg.F, 220 deg.C, gas mark 7 for about 10 minutes, but keep an eye on it.

Place on a serving dish and decorate with whole cranberries and slices of canned pineapple. Serve either hot or cold with cranberry, orange and redcurrant sauce. Serves 10.

Thanksgiving Turkey

Stuffing:
2 oz (50 g) dried apricots, chopped
6 oz (175 g) bacon pieces, chopped
1 large onion, chopped
2 sticks celery, finely sliced
4 oz (100 g) brown breadcrumbs
8 oz (225 g) pork sausagemeat
3 oz (75 g) pine nuts
2 good tablespoons chopped parsley
1 teaspoon salt
Plenty of ground black pepper
1 egg, beaten

12 lb (5.4 kg) turkey

Cook's Tip *Turkey with an apricot, bacon and pine nut stuffing. If pine nuts are difficult to get, used sliced blanched almonds.*

First prepare the stuffing: Pour boiling water over the apricots and leave to soak for a couple of hours, drain well. Put the bacon pieces in a non-stick frying pan and cook slowly at first, then drain out the fat and fry the bacon until crisp. Lift out with a slotted spoon and put on one side. Add the onion to the pan, add remaining fat and brown, then mix with all the other stuffing ingredients and use to stuff the breast of the turkey.

Check the weight of the turkey with the stuffing and calculate the cooking time (about 4 hours for this weight).

Heat the oven to 350 deg.F, 180 deg.C, gas mark 4.

Put a large piece of foil in the roasting tin. Lift the turkey onto the foil and season well. Wrap the foil loosely over the bird with the fold at the top. Put the turkey on a shelf just below the middle of the oven and cook for 3 hours, then open the foil, rub the legs and breast with butter and cook for a further 1¼ hours.

Cook the giblets from the turkey in water with an onion and herbs and then use the stock to make a good gravy to serve with the turkey. Serves 12.

Cranberry, Orange and Redcurrant Sauce

8 oz (225 g) cranberries
Grated rind and juice of one small orange
4 tablespoons redcurrant jelly
A little orange liqueur if liked

Put all the ingredients in a saucepan with a tightly fitting lid and cook over a gentle heat until the cranberries are soft, stirring from time to time. Remove from the heat, add a couple of tablespoons of orange liqueur.

Turn into a small dish and serve either hot or cold with Virginia baked ham.

Boston Baked Beans

12 oz (350 g) haricot beans
1 tablespoon black treacle
1 tablespoon golden syrup
2 tablespoons dark soft brown sugar
2 teaspoons dry mustard
2 tablespoons tomato puree
2 teaspoons salt
Ground black pepper

2 large onions
8 oz (225 g) salt belly pork or unsmoked bacon
1 pint (600 ml) water

Cook's Tip *This dish uses one of the cheapest cuts of pork, but needs really long slow cooking. It is ideal if you have an Aga, Rayburn or Esse cooker.*

Wash the beans, put in a bowl and cover with cold water. Leave to soak overnight.

Drain the beans and throw away the water. Rinse beans thoroughly. Put in a saucepan with 1 pint (600 ml) water. Bring to the boil and simmer for 30 minutes. Do not add salt at this stage as it toughens the beans.

Meanwhile take a large 4½ pint (2.5 l) ovenproof casserole and put in the treacle, syrup, sugar, mustard, tomato puree, salt and pepper and stir until well blended. Cut the onions into wedges. Remove the skin from the pork or bacon and cut into ½ inch (1.25 cm) cubes. Add both ingredients to the casserole.

Remove the beans from the heat, do not drain, but add them with the liquid to the casserole. Stir well, cover the casserole and put in a cool oven at 275 deg.F, 140 deg.C, gas mark 1. Cook the beans for 4 to 6 hours, stirring from time to time.

If the dish is too liquid, remove lid towards the end of the cooking time for about 30 minutes. If the dish is too dry add a little extra water.

Serve with garlic bread.
Serves 4.

All-American Iceberg Salad

Iceberg lettuces are more expensive than other kinds, but they are crisp and hearty and go a long way.

1 small Iceberg lettuce
1 bunch watercress
2 oz (50 g) button mushrooms, finely sliced
6 spring onions, chopped
1 red pepper

Dressing:
2 tablespoons mayonnaise
2 tablespoons sour cream
2 tablespoons natural yoghurt
2 tablespoons white wine vinegar
Salt and freshly ground black pepper

Break the lettuce into small pieces and place in a large salad bowl. Break the watercress into small sprigs and add to the bowl with the mushrooms, spring onions and red pepper, which should have the seeds removed and be cut into thin strips. Toss well and then serve with a bowl of dressing. Serves 8.

Fresh Fruit Sorbet

Looks pretty decorated with fresh fruit or sprigs of mint or borage.

1 lb (450 g) raspberries, loganberries, blackcurrants, gooseberries or blackberries or 6 large lemons
6 oz (175 g) caster sugar
½ pint (300 ml) water
2 egg whites

Prepare your chosen fruit as follows: For raspberries and loganberries puree the fruit in an electric blender, then sieve to remove all pips.

For blackcurrants, gooseberries and blackberries, cook the fruit in half the water until tender, cool slightly, then puree in an electric blender or sieve and cool.

For lemons, simply squeeze out the juice.

Now make the syrup: Dissolve the sugar in the water, cool and add to the fruit puree or juice. Pour into a flat shallow tray or container and freeze until a

Boston Baked Beans

mushy consistency. When this stage is reached whisk the egg whites until thick and foamy.

Fold into the mushy fruit mixture. Taste and if liked add lemon juice before freezing until the sorbet is firm. This will take several hours.

Leave to thaw at room temperature for about 15 minutes before scooping out to serve. Serves 8.

Carrot Cake

This is gooey and delicious.

8 oz (225 g) self-raising flour
2 level teaspoons baking powder
5 oz (150 g) light soft brown sugar
2 oz (50 g) walnuts, chopped
4 oz (100 g) carrots, washed, trimmed and grated
2 ripe bananas, mashed
2 eggs
¼ pint (150 ml) salad or corn oil

Topping:
3 oz (75 g) soft butter or margarine
3 oz (75 g) rich cream cheese
6 oz (175 g) icing sugar, sieved
½ teaspoon vanilla essence

Heat the oven to 350 deg.F, 180 deg.C, gas mark 4. Grease and line with greased greaseproof paper an 8 inch (20 cm) round cake tin.

Sift together the flour and baking powder into a large bowl and stir in the sugar. Add the nuts, carrots and bananas and mix lightly. Make a well in the centre and add the eggs and oil. Beat well until thoroughly blended.

Turn into the tin and bake in the oven for about 1¼ hours until golden brown. When cooked the cake will have shrunk slightly from the sides of the tin and a warm skewer pierced into the centre of it will come out clean. Turn out the cake and remove the paper and then leave to cool on a wire rack.

Topping: Place all the ingredients together in a bowl and beat well until blended and smooth. Spread over the cake and rough up with a fork. Leave in a cool place to harden slightly before serving.

Pecan Pie

Cook's Tip *If you can't get pecans, which are very expensive, use walnuts.*

Pastry:
4 oz (100 g) plain flour
2 oz (50 g) butter
1 oz (25 g) lard
1 egg yolk
½ oz (12.5 g) caster sugar
1 teaspoon water

Filling:
1 oz (25 g) butter
6 oz (175 g) soft brown sugar
3 eggs
8 oz (227 g) jar maple syrup or 5 oz (150 g) golden syrup mixed with a tablespoon black treacle and made up to 8 oz (225 g) with boiling water
1 teaspoon vanilla esence
¼ teaspoon salt
3 oz (75 g) pecans, halved

Make the pastry: Put the flour in a bowl, add the fats cut in small pieces and rub in with the fingertips until the mixture resembles fine breadcrumbs. Mix the egg yolk, sugar and water together, stir into the dry ingredients and bind together. Wrap in cling film and chill in the refrigerator for 30 minutes.

Heat the oven to 425 deg.F, 220 deg.C, gas mark 7. Roll out the pastry on a floured table and line an 8 inch (20 cm) loose-bottomed deep flan tin. Line the flan with greaseproof paper and baking beans and bake blind for 10 minutes. Remove the paper and beans and return the flan to the oven for a further 5 minutes to dry out the base.

For the filling: Cream butter and sugar together, whisk the eggs and add to the creamed mixture with the maple syrup, vanilla essence and salt. Beat well. Arrange the nuts over the base of the flan flat side down.

Pour in the filling and bake in the oven turned down to 375 deg.F, 190 deg.C, gas mark 5 for about 40 minutes. The pie will

Pecan Pie

have risen but will fall back on cooling.

Leave to cool but serve slightly warm with cream. Serves 6.

American Cheesecake

A rich cheesecake that's delicious even without the topping.

Flan case:
3 oz (75 g) butter
1½ oz (40 g) demerara sugar
6 oz (175 g) Digestive biscuits, crushed

Filling:
4 oz (100 g) cream cheese
Juice of 1½ lemons
½ pint (300 ml) double cream, lightly whipped with a little sugar to taste

Topping:
6 oz (175 g) strawberries
4 tablespoons redcurrant jelly

For the flan case: Melt the butter in a saucepan, stir in the sugar and crushed biscuits and mix very well. Press over the base and sides of an 8 inch (20 cm) flan ring on a plate or a loose bottomed flan tin, using a metal spoon.

For the filling: Cream the cheese with the lemon juice and a little whipped cream until soft and then fold in the remaining cream. Turn into the flan case and leave in a cool place to set.

Hull and halve the strawberries and arrange on top.

Heat the redcurrant jelly in a small saucepan until it has melted and then carefully spoon or brush over the strawberries. Leave to set. Serves 6.

Brownies

The high proportion of sugar is traditional in this recipe. Americans have a sweet tooth!

1½ oz (40 g) cocoa
About 5 tablespoons water
3 oz (75 g) margarine
2 eggs
8 oz (225 g) caster sugar
3½ oz (87 g) plain flour
½ level teaspoon baking powder
Pinch of salt

Brownies

2 oz (50 g) walnuts, roughly chopped

Heat the oven to 350 deg.F, 180 deg.C, gas mark 4. Line with greased greaseproof paper an oblong tin 11 inches by 7 inches by 1 inch deep (27.5 by 17.5 by 2.5 cm).

Mix the cocoa with the water in a small saucepan till smooth, add the margarine and heat gently until it has melted and the mixture is a thick cream. Remove from the heat.

Whisk the eggs and sugar together until light and then whisk in the cocoa mixture.

Sift the flour with the baking powder and salt and fold into the cake with the nuts. Turn into the tin and bake in the oven for 35 to 40 minutes.

When cooked the Brownies will have shrunk slightly from the sides of the tin and have a pale crust on top.

Leave to cool in the tin and then peel off the paper and cut into 15 pieces. Makes 15 Brownies.

Texas She Cake

An interesting regional version of the traditional American brownies.

2 level tablespoons cocoa
¼ pint (150 ml) less 2 tablespoons water
4 oz (100 g) soft margarine
7 oz (200 g) caster sugar
4 oz (100 g) plain flour
¼ teaspoon salt
1 egg, beaten
2 rounded tablespoons soured cream
½ teaspoon bicarbonate of soda
½ teaspoon vanilla essence

Icing:
2 oz (50 g) margarine
2 level tablespoons cocoa
3 tablespoons milk
8 oz (225 g) icing sugar, sieved

Heat the oven to 375 deg.F, 190 deg.C, gas mark 5. Grease and line with greased greaseproof paper a cake tin 11 by 7 by 1½ inches (27.5 by 17.5 by 3.5 cm) deep.

Put the cocoa, water and margarine in a small saucepan. Place over a moderate heat and bring to the boil, stirring, so that the margarine has melted. Remove from the heat and cool.

Put the sugar, flour and salt in a bowl, make a well in the centre and add the chocolate mixture, egg, soured cream, bicarbonate of soda and vanilla essence. Mix well and then turn into the tin and bake for 20 minutes.

Meanwhile prepare the icing: Put the margarine, cocoa and milk in a saucepan and bring to the boil, stirring, so that the margarine melts. Remove from the heat, add the icing sugar and mix well.

As soon as the cake comes out of the oven spread it with the icing so that it soaks into the cake. Leave to cool in the tin and then cut into 16 pieces and store in an airtight tin.

MEXICO

Many of Mexico's foods have been exported and are cultivated elsewhere, but beans, chillies, vanilla, chocolate, avocado pears, cashews, peanuts, tomatoes and aubergines still remain characteristic of genuine Mexican cooking. Their staple crop is maize, which was originally grown in the ancient Mayan civilisation. This forms the basis of their diet, along with beans and chillies. Mexico abounds in oregano (wild marjoram), mint, celery, anise and cloves. Wild herbs and spices are used to flavour thick stews of beans and meat traditionally cooked in clay pots. Many dishes are eaten with tortillas, thin pancakes used as an edible scoop. Leftovers are rolled in remaining tortillas and fried for the next meal. In place of puddings, the Mexicans serve fresh fruit, especially watermelon, and delicious soft drinks made from them.

Gaspacho

A refreshing soup for a summer's day. It contrasts pleasantly with the hot spicy flavours of many Mexican main dishes.

2 x 14 oz (397 g) cans tomatoes
1 small onion, peeled
1 small green pepper, seeds and pith removed
½ cucumber, peeled
2 small cloves garlic, crushed
2 slices white bread, crusts removed
Salt
Freshly ground black pepper
3 tablespoons wine vinegar
3 tablespoons salad oil
A few drops of Tabasco sauce
½ pint (300 ml) water
3 teaspoons caster sugar

Chop the vegetables roughly, then place all the ingredients together in an electric blender and puree until smooth. Do this in several batches and then mix together in a large bowl.

Chill in the refrigerator for two or three hours, then taste and check seasoning.

Mexican Bean Salad and Chilli Con Carne

Serve the soup very cold with an ice cube in each bowl with side dishes of cubed cucumber, chopped red and green pepper mixed with chopped onion and fried croutons all served in separate dishes. Serves 4 to 6.

Chilli Con Carne

6 oz (175 g) mixed red kidney and black eyed beans
2 onions
2 cloves garlic
2 green peppers
3 tablespoons oil
1 lb (450 g) good minced beef
14 oz (397 g) can peeled tomatoes
¼ pint (150 ml) beef stock
1 level teaspoon chilli powder, less if you like it mild
1 level teaspoon paprika pepper
2 level teaspoons salt

Cook's Tip *This is best made 12 hours ahead, then the ingredients blend well and the beans absorb the spicy flavours. Use a well known make of chilli powder according to taste.*

Put the beans in a bowl, cover with cold water and leave to soak overnight.

Chop the onions and crush the garlic, remove the seeds from the green peppers and cut into chunky pieces. Heat the oil in a pan, add onions, garlic, green pepper and beef. Fry for 10 minutes, stirring continuously.

Add tomatoes, stock, chilli powder, paprika pepper and salt and bring to the boil, stirring. Drain the beans and rinse thoroughly, then stir into the pan. Cover and simmer for about one hour or until the beans and mince are tender. Taste and check seasoning.

Serve with chunky pieces of bread and a green salad.

If made in advance, this dish needs to be reheated in a hot oven for about 30 minutes until piping hot, or over a moderate heat on a hob stirring occasionally until hot through. Serves 6.

Mexican Bean Salad

A great change from the usual rice or potato salad. It is essential to soak the beans overnight first.

1 lb (450 g) mixed dried beans; could include haricot, red kidney, black eye and aduki

Crushed garlic
A little finely chopped onion
4 sticks celery, finely chopped
French dressing
Chopped parsley

Put the beans in a bowl, cover with cold water and leave to soak overnight.

Drain well and put in a saucepan, cover with cold water and bring to the boil. Simmer for one hour or until tender. Rinse under hot water and while they are still warm put in a bowl and add the other ingredients. Toss well, season and then cover. Leave in a cool place to marinate overnight.

Turn into a serving dish, sprinkle with parsley before serving. Serves 4 to 6.

Eggs Flamenca

A colourful dish that makes a tasty informal lunch or supper. This dish can also be cooked in individual dishes in the oven.

1 tablespoon olive oil
2 large onions, sliced
2 large tomatoes
4 oz (100 g) bacon, chopped
Salt and pepper
2 small canned red peppers
4 oz (100 g) chorizo sausage, thinly sliced (optional)
4 eggs
4 oz (100 g) peeled prawns (optional)

Put the oil in a frying pan or heatproof serving dish, add the onions and cook for 10 minutes or until tender.

Put the tomatoes in a pan of boiling water and leave for a minute, then remove with a spoon and carefully peel off the skin and cut each tomato in slices. Add to the onions with the bacon and cook for a further 10 minutes. Season well. Stir in the red pepper and arrange the sausage slices around the edge of the pan.

Make 4 holes in the mixture and break an egg into each. Cook for 3 to 4 minutes or until the whites have set and the yolk is still soft.

Sprinkle over the prawns if used and serve at once from the pan in which it was cooked. Serves 2 or 4.

Eggs Flamenca

Guacomola

1 level teaspoon salt
¼ level teaspoon freshly ground black pepper
1 level teaspoon made mustard
2 level teaspoons caster sugar
6 tablespoons salad oil
2 tablespoons lemon juice
2 ripe avocado pears
2 tomatoes, skinned, seeded and chopped
4 spring onions, chopped

Put the salt, pepper, mustard and sugar into a small bowl. Blend in the oil a little at a time, then blend in the lemon juice.

Cut the avocado pears in half, remove the stones and scoop out the flesh into another bowl. Mash with a fork until quite smooth.

Blend in the dressing slowly and then finally fold in the tomato and spring onion.

Turn the guacomola into a dish and serve with chilli con carne or as a dip with crisp raw vegetables.

Cook's Tip *If you have to leave your avocados once mashed, put the stones back into the flesh to stop it discolouring.*

Tortillas

1 lb (450 g) strong white flour
2 level teaspoons baking powder
1 level teaspoon salt
About ½ pint (300 ml) less 2 tablespoons warm water

Measure the flour, baking powder and salt into a bowl, make a well in the centre and gradually add the warm water, mixing well to form a firm dough. Add a little extra water if necessary. Turn onto a clean surface and knead until smooth. Place in a polythene bag and leave for 20 minutes.

Divide the dough into 12 pieces and then press each piece flat and roll out to a very thin round about 10 inches (25 cm) in diameter.

Lightly oil a heavy frying pan and put on quite a high heat, add a tortilla and cook until bubbles

Mexican Chicken and Tortillas

appear. Then turn over and cook until a pale golden colour on the other side.

Stack in a folded towel until all the tortillas are cooked and then serve buttered and rolled up. Makes 12 tortillas.

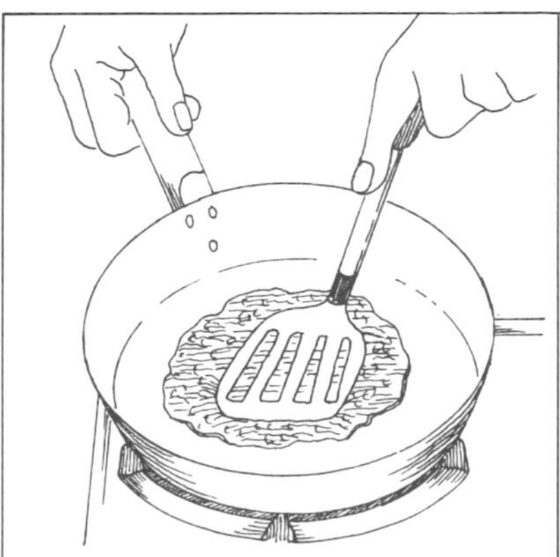

Flatten the Tortilla with a fish slice while it is frying.

Cook's Tip *In Mexico tortillas are served instead of bread or rolls. Any that are left over may be cut in triangles and fried in hot oil until golden brown and crisp.*

Mexican Chicken

This is a colourful dish and looks good served on a large, brightly patterned plate. Rice is a good accompaniment.

4 chicken joints
3 tablespoons olive oil
2 large onions, sliced
2 cloves garlic
14 oz (397 g) can peeled tomatoes
¼ pint (150 ml) chicken stock
1 bouquet garni
Salt and pepper
2 red peppers, sliced
1 oz (25 g) fresh white breadcrumbs
12 stuffed green olives (optional)

Heat the oil in a large pan and fry the joints quickly to brown on both sides. Lift out and put on a plate.

Add the onions and garlic to the pan and fry for 5 minutes. Add tomatoes, stock, bouquet garni and seasoning with most of the red peppers, reserving just a few slices for garnish.

Return the chicken joints to the pan, cover and simmer for 30 minutes, or until the chicken is tender.

Lift out the chicken, place on a serving dish and keep warm. Remove the bouquet garni and stir the breadcrumbs into the pan. Puree the sauce in one or two batches in a blender. Rinse out the saucepan, return the sauce to it and reheat, taste and check seasoning. Stir in the olives and spoon over the chicken, garnish with the remaining rings of red pepper. Serves 4.

INDIA

The best of Indian cooking offers a delicate balance of subtle flavours which enhances, rather than disguises the taste of the natural ingredients.

Many Hindus are strict vegetarians and Muslims are forbidden all pork products, but the great variety of fruit, vegetables and cereals makes up for these restrictions. Rice is the staple food, and the unpolished variety is more nutritious. In the north and west they eat chapattis, made from wheat and maize, and everywhere yoghurt is a common accompaniment to meals. Its coolness contrasts pleasingly with any spicy dish.

When making a curry, fry your spices gently to avoid making them pungent or bitter. Indian cooks use ghee (clarified butter), but vegetable oil or your usual cooking medium will provide very satisfactory results.

Mild Authentic Indian Curry

This recipe was given to me by Fatima Lakhani as a curry that her family has enjoyed for generations. It is not over-poweringly strong, has a superb flavour, a rich deep colour and is surprisingly simple to make. It freezes well so make more than you need. Thaw slowly before reheating.

The spices:
2 rounded tablespoons ground coriander
1 rounded teaspoon ground cumin
1 level teaspoon ground turmeric
1 rounded teaspoon Garam Masala, (ground mixed spices) *Or* instead of the above use 3 rounded tablespoons curry powder
2 fat cloves garlic, crushed
Piece fresh green ginger, size of a walnut, finely chopped
2 teaspoons salt

3 tablespoons corn oil
2 large onions, chopped
8 oz (227 g) can peeled tomatoes
2 generous tablespoons tomato puree
2 lb (900 g) chuck steak, cut into cubes
½ pint (300 ml) water
Fresh mango slices (optional)

First mix the spices together and then add the garlic, ginger and salt.

Cook's Tip *If you like a really hot curry add chilli powder with the spices. Half a teaspoon of ground chilli is enough for most tastes.*

Take a heavy pan, measure in the oil, add the onions and fry until an even golden brown. Take care not to let them catch and brown as this would spoil the flavour. Add all the spice mixture, tomatoes and tomato puree and cook over a medium heat, without a lid, stirring until the oil starts to come through slightly. Then add the meat, cover with a lid and simmer for 15 minutes. Remove the lid, add water, cover and bring to the boil and simmer gently for about 2½ hours or until the meat is tender.

Garnish with fresh mango slices if you can get them brushed with lemon juice to prevent discolouration. Serves 6.

Accompaniments for Curry

Rice
Use basmati rice or long grained rice and cook in plenty of salted water until just tender. Drain well and allow about 2 oz (50 g) rice per person.

Indian pilau rice bought in packets is a yellow spiced saffron rice and adds variety.

Poppodums fried in deep fat and served in a stack are also put on the table.

Sambols (side dishes)

Cucumber, yoghurt and mint:
Mix a tablespoon chopped mint with 3 inches (7.5 cm) diced cucumber and ¼ pint (150 ml) carton yoghurt. Season well.
Banana:
2 bananas, sliced and tossed in lemon juice.
Onion and green pepper:
1 mild onion, finely sliced, mixed with chopped green pepper.
Mango chutney:
Buy this ready-made.

Mild Authentic Indian Curry, Dahl, Poppodum and Sambols

Tandoori Chicken

Also if liked, serve hardboiled egg slices, mixed salted nuts, tomato slices and coconut in separate dishes.

Great curry enthusiasts will also like dahl, a spiced lentil dish, and chapattis, unlevened bread, bought from Indian shops.

If you find the taste too hot, natural yoghurt stirred in will help.

Dahl

8 oz (225 g) green lentils
1 bayleaf
2 tablespoons oil
1 large carrot, chopped
1 large green pepper, chopped
1 large onion, chopped
1 clove garlic, crushed
½ inch (1.25 cm) piece fresh root ginger
½ level teaspoon ground cinnamon
½ level teaspoon ground cumin
½ level teaspoon ground coriander
14 oz (397 g) can peeled tomatoes
Salt and pepper

Soak the lentils overnight in cold water, then drain and discard the water. Put the lentils in a saucepan and add sufficient water to cover. Bring to the boil, add the bayleaf and simmer for 30 minutes or until the lentils are tender. Drain and remove the bayleaf.

Heat the oil in a large pan, add the vegetables and fry for 10 minutes, stirring. Then add the lentils, spices and tomatoes and cook gently for 10 minutes or until the carrots are soft.

Discard the ginger, put the mixture in three batches in the blender and puree quickly for about 30 seconds on top speed. The dahl should not be smooth, retaining some texture.

Rinse out the saucepan, reheat the dahl and taste and check seasoning. Serve hot. Serves 4 with pitta bread or about 8 as an accompaniment to curry.

Tandoori Chicken

4 chicken portions
1 level teaspoon salt
Juice of 1 lemon
1 inch (2.5 cm) piece root ginger or ½ teaspoon ground ginger
2 cloves garlic
4 green chillies, if available
A few fresh mint leaves
5 oz (150 ml) carton natural yoghurt
1 teaspoon chilli powder
1 teaspoon ground black pepper
¼ teaspoon ground nutmeg
¼ teaspoon Garam Masala
¼ teaspoon red food colouring (optional)

Cook's Tip *If liked use a packet of Tandoori Barbecue spice mix and make up as directed on the packet.*

Skin the chicken and prick all over with a fork or make small cuts with a sharp knife. Put in a dish and sprinkle with salt and lemon juice. Peel the root ginger and garlic and crush. Finely mince or chop the chillies and mint leaves and add to the ginger and garlic with the remaining ingredients, mix well and pour over the chicken. Cover and leave to marinate overnight.

Remove the rack from the grill pan, lay in the chicken and grill under a hot grill for 5 minutes on each side, then reduce the heat and cook for a further 10 minutes on each side. Serve with lemon wedges on a bed of lettuce and sliced onion. Serves 4.

Lamb Curry

Take care to wash your hands straight away after handling fresh chillies. I have found that should you rub your eyes with your hands it makes them sting like mad.

1½ inch (3.75 cm) piece fresh root ginger, peeled and chopped
3 cloves garlic, peeled
2 green chillies
2 oz (50 g) unsalted cashew nuts
¼ teaspoon ground cloves
¼ teaspoon ground cardamom
2 teaspoons ground coriander
¼ teaspoon ground turmeric
6 tablespoons water
2 oz (50 g) butter
2 onions, finely chopped
2 lb (900 g) lean lamb, cubed
½ pint (300 ml) natural yoghurt
1 tablespoon lemon juice
Salt

Put the ginger, garlic, chillies, nuts and all the spices with the water in a blender and puree until smooth.

Melt the butter in a pan, add the onions and lamb and fry for 5 minutes, then stir in the spice mixture with the yoghurt and mix well, cover the saucepan and simmer gently for one hour.

Stir in the lemon juice and continue cooking for a further 30 minutes or until the lamb is tender. Check seasoning. Serve with plain boiled rice. Serves 6.

Prawn Curry

A quick and easy curry that tastes delicious with really fresh giant prawns.

2 oz (50 g) butter
1 large onion, chopped
1 level teaspoon ground coriander
½ level teaspoon ground cumin
¼ level teaspoon ground turmeric
¼ level teaspoon chilli powder
¼ pint (150 ml) chicken stock
3 large tomatoes, peeled, chopped and the seeds removed
Salt
1-2 tablespoons lemon juice
8 oz (225 g) peeled prawns
2 tablespoons plain yoghurt (optional)

Heat the butter in a saucepan, add the onion and fry for 5 minutes or until golden brown. Stir in all the spices and cook for a minute. Add the stock, tomatoes and a little salt and bring to the boil, then reduce the heat and simmer for 30 minutes.

Stir in the lemon juice and prawns and heat through, stir in the yoghurt if used and taste and check seasoning. Serves 3.

Curry Powder

Buy the spices from an Indian specialist grocer or store. Usually sold in sealed vacuum-packed tins.

Ground coriander	4 parts
Ground cumin	2 parts
Ground turmeric	1 part
Garam Masala	1 part

Add chilli powder to the curry at the cooking time to taste.

Keen curry enthusiasts may make their own Garam Masala from:

Ground cinnamon	2 parts
Ground cloves	1 part
Ground cardamom	1 part

Tropical Indian Fruit Salad

A very easy and suitable dessert to follow curry is a chilled fruit salad.

Buy cans of some tropical fruits. Choose a selection from guavas, pineapple, paw paw, lychees, mandarin oranges and mangoes. These are available from Indian food shops and specialist shops. Mix together in a glass bowl and chill for at least 12 hours. Serve with cream.

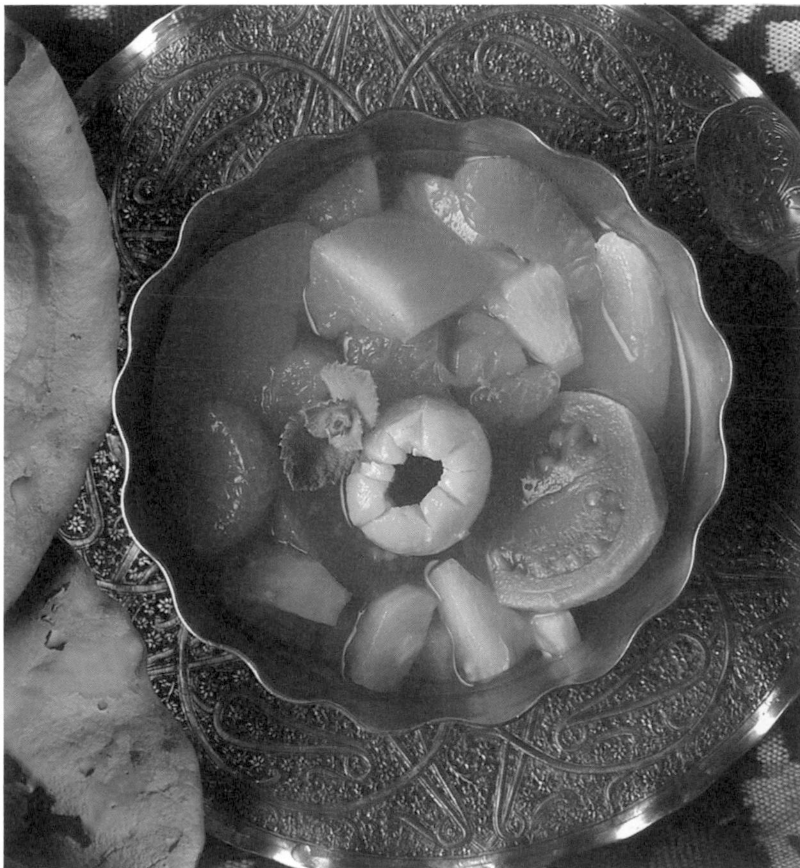

Tropical Indian Fruit Salad

CHINA

In ancient China, eating was the most important form of social entertainment, reaching its peak in hours' long Mandarin banquets. Today, in a very different China, eating is still essentially communal.

Eating with chopsticks means that the food has to be pre-cut into bite-size pieces, and one of the hallmarks of a good Chinese cook is mastery in the art of knifework. However, the major characteristic of Chinese cooking is the unusual way it contrasts tastes and textures and brings together opposites such as sweet and sour, soft and crisp, pungent and bland. Seasoning is the secret: sugar, garlic, spring onions, ginger and especially soy sauce add a distinctive oriental flavour to meat, fish, poultry, nuts and vegetables.

Sweet and Sour Pork

The contrast of sweet and sour flavours is typically Chinese, but easily reproduced in an English kitchen.

Batter:
4 oz (100 g) self-raising flour
½ teaspoon salt
¼ pint (150 ml) water

Sauce:
12 oz (340 g) can pineapple chunks
3 tablespoons malt vinegar
1 tablespoon tomato puree
2 teaspoons soft brown sugar
2 teaspoons cornflour
¼ cucumber, peeled and cut in small dice

Pork mixture:
8 oz (225 g) lean pork, cut in ½ inch (1.25 cm) pieces
Salt and pepper
Oil for deep frying

Beat together the batter ingredients and leave on one side.

Drain the pineapple chunks and put 5 tablespoons of the juice in a saucepan with the vinegar, tomato puree, sugar and cornflour. Bring to the boil, stirring until thickened. Add the cucumber and pineapple chunks.

Season the pork well, dip the pieces in the batter and then fry in hot deep fat for about 3 to 4 minutes until crisp and golden brown and the pork is cooked through. Lift out with a slotted spoon and drain on kitchen paper. Serve piled on a hot dish with the sauce poured over or separately if preferred. Serves 4 with other dishes.

Chicken Chop Suey

Chinese egg noodles are tasty and make this dish fairly substantial.

4 oz (100 g) egg noodles
8 oz (225 g) chicken breast
8 oz (227 g) can whole peeled water chestnuts
2 tablespoons oil
1 small onion, finely chopped
1 carrot, cut in fine strips
¾ inch (2 cm) piece green ginger, very finely chopped
1 tablespoon cornflour
3 tablespoons soy sauce
½ pint (300 ml) chicken stock

Cook the noodles as directed on the packet and rinse and drain well.

Cut the meat in pencil strips, drain the water chestnuts and slice.

Heat the oil in a large shallow pan and stir-fry all the chicken and vegetables for 5 minutes, tossing well. Add the noodles.

Blend the cornflour with the soy sauce and chicken stock and stir into the pan until the sauce thickens. Then reduce the heat and simmer for 10 minutes or until chicken and vegetables are tender.

Taste and check seasoning and serve piled on a hot dish. Serves 4 with other dishes.

Pork, Sweet and Sour with Cashew Nuts

12 oz (350 g) pork fillet
3 tablespoons oil
2 oz (50 g) cashew nuts
8 oz (227 g) can pineapple cubes
1 level tablespoon cornflour
3 tablespoons malt vinegar
1 tablespoon tomato puree
2 tablespoons brown sugar
Salt and pepper

Sweet and Sour Pork with Cashews, Spring Rolls, Chop Suey

Cook's Tip *The Chinese are very partial to nuts. Remember not to buy the salted variety!*

Cut the pork into pencil-thin strips.

Put the oil in a pan and stir-fry the nuts until brown. Lift out onto a plate with a slotted spoon. Add the pork to the pan and stir-fry over a high heat turning all the time for about 2 minutes. Lift out with a slotted spoon onto the plate with the nuts.

Drain the pineapple, reserve 6 tablespoons juice and put in a bowl with the cornflour, vinegar, tomato puree and sugar and mix well.

Pour into the pan and stir over a medium heat until thick. Add the pork and nuts with the pineapple cubes and cook for a minute, taste and add seasoning and serve at once. Serves 6 with other dishes.

Spring Rolls

Filling:
1 tablespoon oil
1 oz (25 g) sliced almonds
4 oz (100 g) mushrooms, chopped
14 oz (397 g) can beansprouts, drained
1 tablespoon soy sauce
1 teaspoon cornflour
2 teaspoons water
Salt and pepper

10-12 unsugared pancakes (see page 11).
1 egg, beaten
Deep oil for frying
Spring onion flowers to decorate

Cook's Tip *To make spring onion flowers, cut the onions to about the size of a short cigarette. Cut through the onion to within 1 inch (2.5 cm) of the root in several places to give a frayed effect. Put in iced water to curl.*

For the filling: Heat the oil in a pan and toss the almonds until slightly browned. Add the mushrooms with the bean-sprouts and soy sauce, toss and cook gently for 2 minutes. Blend the cornflour with the water and stir into the pan and cook for a minute. Season to taste.

Lay the pancakes flat on a work surface and put a tablespoon of the filling in the centre of each. Brush the edges with beaten egg, fold in the sides and then roll up like little parcels.

Deep fat fry for about 3 minutes until golden brown and crisp. Lift out with a slotted spoon and drain on kitchen paper. Makes 10-12 spring rolls.

How to use chopsticks

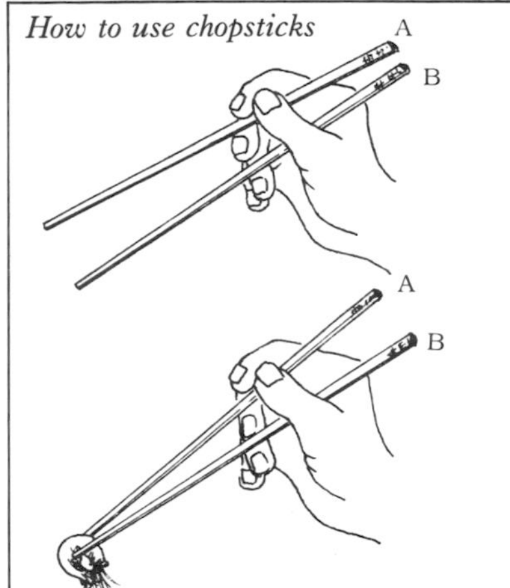

Hold a) between the first and second fingers, pen-style. Hold b) between the second and third fingers and use the chopsticks pincer-fashion to pick up the food. It helps to hold your plate or dish near to your mouth.

Stir-fry Prawns

Stir-Fry Prawns

3 spring onions
2 level teaspoons cornflour
2 tablespoons sherry.
2 tablespoons corn oil
12 oz (350 g) bean sprouts
1 clove garlic, crushed
¼ pint (150 ml) chicken stock
2 tablespoons soy sauce
Salt and ground black pepper
8 oz (225 g) peeled prawns

Cut the spring onions into strips lengthwise, then into 2 inch (5 cm) lengths. Slake the cornflour with the sherry.

Heat the oil in a wok or a large heavy pan until very hot. Add the bean sprouts, spring onions and garlic. Toss well for a few minutes, add the stock and soy sauce with the slaked cornflour and seasoning. Continue cooking and tossing for a further minute and then add the prawns. Heat through for a last minute or until the liquid is creamy and the vegetables still crisp.

Serve with boiled rice or just on its own. Serves 4.

Cook's Tip *You may want to try this recipe with chicken cut into bite-sized pieces if you can't get prawns.*

Fried Rice

This is a tasty rice dish and a pleasant alternative to plain boiled rice, which you can serve as well.

6 oz (175 g) long grain rice
2 tablespoons oil
1 onion, finely diced
4 oz (100 g) streaky bacon, diced
1 egg, beaten
1 level teaspoon caster sugar
½ teaspoon salt
1 tablespoon spring onions, cut into short lengths
1 tablespoon soy sauce

Cook the rice in boiling salted water for about 12 minutes or as directed on the packet. Drain and rinse well.

Heat the oil in a frying pan and fry the onion and bacon gently for about 5 minutes so that the fat runs out of the bacon. Stir in the rice and beaten egg and fry for 2 minutes. Add the sugar, salt and the spring onions with the soy sauce and mix thoroughly until hot.

Taste and check seasoning and serve piled on a hot dish. Serves 4 to 6.

Chinese Dessert Fruits

Crispy Noodles

This is something that children will love. The Chinese also serve soft noodles, boiled.

4 oz (100 g) egg noodles
Corn oil for deep fat frying

Cook the noodles in boiling salted water for about 5 to 6 minutes, strain and rinse in warm water.

Heat the oil in a deep pan until hot (375 deg.F, 190 deg.C). To test whether the oil is hot enough, drop a small cube of bread into it, which should brown in about 3 seconds.

Place the noodles in a wire basket and lower into the pan, lifting out for a moment if the fat foams up. Lower again and repeat the action until the fat has calmed down. Cook until pale golden, and drain on kitchen paper. Serves 4 with other dishes.

Chinese Dessert Fruits

Combine the melon and lychees the day before and chill well. Just before serving add the ginger and kiwi fruit.

1 Galia or honeydew melon
1 can lychees
A few pieces of stem ginger in syrup
1 kiwi fruit

Cut the melon in half and remove all the seeds. Scoop ball shapes out of the melon with a melon baller. Put in a bowl with the contents of a can of lychees, cover and chill.

Slip the melon cases into a polythene bag and chill ready to use as a container for the fruit.

Next day add a few pieces of chopped stem ginger, about 3 tablespoons. Peel the kiwi fruit and slice and add to the fruit. Blend well and pile into the melon shells.

Serve chilled with no cream. Decorate with a fresh flower if you like. Serves 6.

JAPAN

Japanese food varies greatly from that of China. It is unparalleled in its delicacy and simplicity: there are no heavy sauces and spices are light. Presentation is imaginative and highly attractive, but the basic ingredients are left in as natural a state as possible It is probably this natural approach plus the fact that the Japanese eat slowly, taking a leisurely pause between one dish and the next in a long succession of courses, that makes them one of the healthiest races in the world. Even if you don't fancy eating slivers of raw fish, it's worth taking a tip from the Japanese when it comes to cooking vegetables: they like them very fresh and barely cooked, so that they retain all their natural crispness. Drink rice wine (sake) or green tea with a Japanese meal, and follow it with a piece of fresh fruit.

Tempura

Tempura means to cover in a light batter and then deep fat fry. It is a method used mostly with vegetables and prawns.

12 whole prawns

Batter:
4 oz (100 g) plain flour
½ teaspoon salt
1 egg
¼ pint (150 ml) water

Vegetables:
8 okra
2 courgettes, sliced
8 fresh asparagus tips
¼ cauliflower or broccoli in sprigs
4 oz (100 g) button mushrooms
Oil for frying
Cornflour

Tendashi sauce (hot sauce):
2 tablespoons soy sauce
2 tablespoons sake (rice wine)
¼ pint (150 ml) chicken stock
1 teaspoon sugar

Shell the prawns leaving on the tails and then wash thoroughly.

Make the batter: Measure flour and salt into a bowl, making a well in the centre. Blend the egg with the water and then gradually add to the flour and beat to a smooth batter.

Pour 1 inch (2.5 cm) of vegetable oil into a pan and heat until it is hot enough to crisp a drop of batter immediately. Lightly dust the vegetables and prawns with cornflour (this helps the batter to stay on during cooking) and then dip them in the batter. Put straight into the hot oil and fry for 2-3 minutes until batter is golden brown and puffy. Lift out with a slotted spoon and drain on kitchen paper.

For the sauce: Mix together all the ingredients, heat through and put in a small bowl.

Pile the tempura on a plate and serve with the sauce. Serves 4.

Yakitori

2 large chicken breasts
24 button mushrooms

Sauce:
5 tablespoons Japanese soy sauce
2 tablespoons white sugar
1 tablespoon water
1 tablespoon rice wine

***Cook's Tip** These are Japanese-style kebabs served on a skewer. If you can't get Japanese soy sauce you can use light soy sauce*

Remove the skin and bone from the chicken and cut into small bite size pieces. Place four pieces of chicken and 3 mushrooms alternately on a skewer, starting and finishing with a piece of chicken.

Mix all the sauce ingredients together in a saucepan and bring to the boil for 3 minutes, until slightly reduced, then cool. Marinate the kebabs in the sauce for 30 minutes and then cook under a hot grill for about 5 minutes, turning frequently and basting with the sauce until they turn golden brown and the sugar starts to caramelize. Take care not to overbrown.

Serve on plates, two per person and garnish with a sprig of parsley. Serves 4.

Japanese Style Trout

This recipe may also be cooked

Yakitori, Tempura and Tendashi Sauce with Sake

outside on a barbeque.

4 trout
Butter
Salt

Wash the trout and clean thoroughly but leave the head and tail on. Make 2 cuts each side. Take 4 long fine skewers and starting at the tail pass the skewer through the fish just below the back bone, then bring the skewer back to the front of the fish. Finally pass through just below the gills so that the fish is made into an S shape.

Remove the rack from the grill pan and heat the grill to moderate. Place a little butter in the pan and melt, then add the fish and brush with the butter, sprinkle with salt and grill for about 8 to 10 minutes, turning once. Serves 4.

Sukiyaki

Sukiyaki can be cooked at the table using a fondue cooker. To eat in the Japanese style each person breaks a raw egg into a bowl beating lightly with chopsticks, then the beef and vegetables are then dipped into the egg and eaten.

1 lb (450 g) rump or sirloin steak
Vegetable oil

Sauce:
6 tablespoons Japanese soy sauce
4 oz (50 g) granulated sugar
4 tablespoons sake (rice wine)
4 tablespoons chicken stock

Vegetables:
8 spring onions, chopped
1 onion, cut in rings
4 oz (100 g) button mushrooms, sliced
4 small carrots, cut in half and then in matchsticks
10 oz (275 g) shirataki noodles
10 oz (275 g) bean sprouts

Cook's Tip *In Japan they use a little beef suet to rub round the pan first, but this is difficult to get so use vegetable oil instead. If rice wine is not available use white wine or double the amount of stock.*

Freeze the meat for 30 minutes, until it is firm enough to enable you to cut it into wafer thin slices about 1½ inches (3.75 cm) square.

Gently heat a large heavy frying pan or wok and run the oil around the base. Add the meat slices and brown on each side, lift the meat out and arrange on a heatproof dish. Place the sauce ingredients in the frying pan and boil for 5 minutes, to reduce by half. Add the vegetables and cook rapidly for about 5 minutes to lightly cook – they should remain crisp. Taste and add a little more soy sauce if more flavour is needed, or if the liquid in the pan has evaporated add a little more stock and sake.

Arrange the vegetables on the serving dish with the meat, spoon over the small amount of sauce. Serve with plain boiled rice. Serves 4.

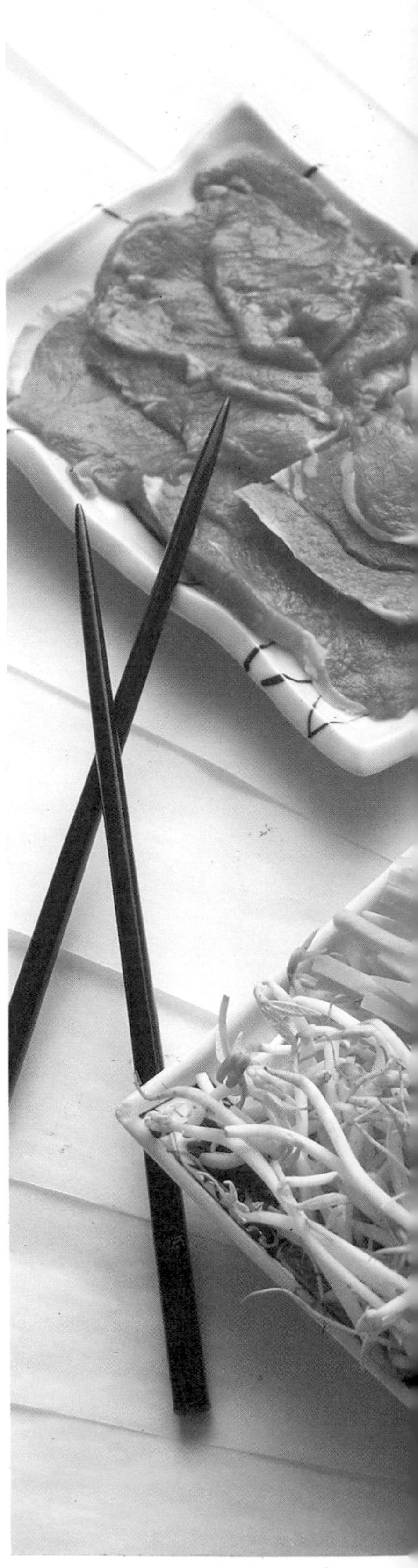

Right: Sukiyaki; Above: Japanese Style Trout

List of Suppliers

Cheong Leen Supermarket
4-10 Tower Street
Cambridgeshire Close
London WC2

Loong Fung Provisions
42/43 Gerrard Street
London W1

Chung Nam Provisions
162 Bromsgrove Street
Birmingham 5

Chung Wah Trading Centre
31/32 Great Georges Square
Liverpool 1